720.9 Mathe, Jean
MAT
      Great buildings and
      monuments of the
      world
      FEB
      1984

GREAT BUILDINGS AND MONUMENTS OF THE WORLD

Text by

JEAN MATHÉ

Translated by
Evelyn Rossiter

Minerva

Cover pages: Hohenschwangau, one of the castles of the Bavarian King Louis II. Title page: the remains of the columns at Persepolis.

Designed and Produced
by Editions Minerva SA

© Editions Minerva SA, Genève, 1982
Printed in Italy

ISBN 0-517-356155

THE PYRAMIDS

The Golden Age of the pyramids stretches over the five centuries, from 2680 to 2180, which make up the Old Kingdom. All the pharaohs of the third to the sixth Dynasties were buried in monumental pyramid-shaped tombs. Until that time the burial-places of kings or dignitaries were known as mastabas: these were modest though carefully built chambers, partly underground, which were adorned with low-reliefs depicting the life of the deceased. As land around Thebes, the new capital, began to become scarce, the tombs were dug into the rock-faces of the famous Valley of the Kings.

The construction of a pyramid of the High Period (third millenium and fourth dynasty) had to comply with all sorts of traditional requirements, both ritual and practical. The choice of the site was fundamental. It had to be close enough to the capital city of Memphis, and, most importantly, it had to be close to the Nile: as the huge blocks of cut stone were moved over water, the sites of the pyramids were rarely more than half a mile from the highest point of the flood waters, and sometimes only 300 yards—a fact which greatly simplified the painful process of transport. Moreover, all the tombs had to be on the left bank of the Nile, the side on which the sun set: the Shore of the Dead. The only members of the world of the living who were allowed to live there were the craftsmen and embalmers preparing the tombs and the bodies to be placed in them.

Once a site had been chosen, an area of about 300 yards square had to be leveled off, with a degree of accuracy which now seems astonishing: a maximum variation in elevation of 1/2 inch between opposing corners. Care was taken to leave a rocky outcrop in the center of this area, as a core for the future structure. Then a paved road had to be built for the transport of the blocks, which were moved on sleds placed on wooden rollers. Then construction could begin.

The big pyramids took twenty years to build, with 4,000 permanent workers living on the

site, and 100,000 workers from July to October, during the Nile flood, as the site was then made more accessible and labor which could not be employed in the fields became available.

In most cases more than two million blocks weighing two to fiftees tons were used. A team of eight men sufficed to transport and lay one block, using ramps which were later demolished. In this way more than 100,000 blocks were moved into position each year; the amount of debris generated in the process equalled more than a half of the final volume of the pyramid.

It seems likely that completed pyramids were colored, though they are always shown as white in polychrome low reliefs. The strict orientation of each face, based on the points of the compass, has given rise to numerous fanciful and esoteric theories.

There would appear to be two answers: first, the pyramid was seen as being a stairway enabling the deceased to reach heaven, like the *ziggurat* of ancient Mesopotamia, which linked the earth to the gods. Also, the symbol of the sun-god is a cone or a pyramid, doubtless a physical expression of the sun's rays falling from heaven to earth.

Lef: the pyramids of Gizeh. Above: close-up of the pyramids' exterior.

Nearly 80 pyramids have been counted in Egypt. But the group at Giza is the most perfect example of all. The pyramid-tombs of the great pharaohs of the fourth dynasty occupy a vast platform over a mile square. The pyramid of Mykerinos is the smallest (325 ft square); that of Kephren, which is much bigger (690 ft square) still has part of its original limestone cladding at its top. The oldest and biggest of all, however, is the pyramid of Cheops (750 ft square, and originally 475 ft tall).

Inside the pyramid a number of galleries lead first to the Queen's Chamber, which is actually a mere hint at the royal tomb itself. The plan having been changed for reasons of security, the real King's Chamber is situated at the end of a long ascending gallery 150 ft long, 23 ft wide and 30 ft high.

Despite all the precautions which were taken—fake galleries, blocks sealing off the corridors—all of the pyramids were despoiled.

In his tomb deep inside the pyramid, the dead pharaoh was left alone with his gods. As for the Sphinx, which was carved by the builders working for Cheops out of a rocky outcrop found on the site, its haughty face, scarred by innumerable sandstorms, stares enigmatically at the motley crowds of tourists who have come, 5,000 years later, to visit his master.

THEBES

During the Old Kingdom, Thebes was only a modest hamlet, far removed in every sense from the lavish splendor of Memphis, the venerable capital of the early dynasties. Yet greatness was thrust upon it by the fact of its geographical position, half-way up the Nile, in an amphitheater of arid mountains: it was precisely what the pharaohs needed at a time when they were seeking to unify Upper and Lower Egypt. Therefore, in the XIII dynasty (2000 BC) it became the capital of unified Egypt.

Thenceforth it became powerful and prosperous and was, for more than six centuries, the most prestigious capital city in the ancient world. Its temples, which are among the most superb and the most famous in Egypt, date from this period.

Throughout its entire length, the left bank of the Nile was, for ancient Egyptians, the 'bank of the dead'. The Theban necropolis, the most famous in Antiquity, was carved out of the arid and desolate rock face which emerges from a fringe of palm-trees. For six centuries the pha-raohs buried their tombs in the arid faces of a hostile and steep gorge: the Valley of the Kings. It thus contains 62 cave-tombs lined with low relief sculptures and accessible by means of tunnels.

Despite all the precautions which were taken, the entire necropolis was looted during the pharaonic period. Only the tomb of Tutenkh-amen, which was not discovered until 1922, still contained an admirable set of funeral furniture; its fame, notwithstanding its small size, was thereby assured.

Apart from their tombs, which they would have liked to keep sealed and hidden for eternity, the pharaohs also built funeral temples on the slopes leading to the mountain. Almost all of these now consist of nothing more than fairly uninspiring ruins. At Deir-el-Bahari, however, there is one highly impressive and majestic building: the restored temple of Queen Hatshepsut, the regent of the kingdom from 1505 to 1484. Perfection of layout is here combined with harmonious and powerful proportions, the whole being exceptionally well integrated into its marvelous geological setting.

THE COLOSSI OF MEMNON

Their massive and imposing silhouette faces the rising sun at the edge of the desert, against the desolate ochre backdrop of the clif-flike necropolis of ancient Thebes. Standing on a plinth 7 1/2 ft high, both of them are seated in a frozen, hieratic posture, their hands on their knees. From a height of fifty feet these two crudely carved blocks of pink sandstone stare down at the crowds of tourists which nowadays enliven the once-tranquil Shores of the Dead. The funeral temple of their master, Amenophis III, which had been buried behind them in a cave sunk into the Valley of the Kings, the entrance to which was flanked by the two Colossi, has completely disappeared; it was probably razed by the memorable earthquake of the year 27 AD. All that remains of it is a sandstone stele dedicating the building to Amon.

The Colossi were erected some time around 1400 BC, in the middle of the 18th Dynasty. They were quite a technical feat at the time as each of them was carved from a single block of the finest sandstone in Egypt.

According to a Greek legend reported by Homer, Memnon, the mythical king of Ethiopia and son of the Dawn, having been killed by Achilles, came back to life each morning when his mother caressed his lifeless face with the first ray's of the rising sun. When the rising sun began to heat this gaping hole in its sandstone body, the wounded Colossus emitted a musical sound.

For nearly two centuries, travelers from all over the ancient world went on pilgrimages to see the Colossus. Emperor Hadrian and Empress Sabina made the journey in 130 from Rome so as to able to listen, at daybreak, to the stone singing as the sun's rays grew steadily more brilliant. But all of this stopped the day when Septimus Severus, seeking to restore its original form, repaired the statue, thus silencing its voice.

Since then the patched-up Colossus has sung no more. Like its brother, it still has, carved into its flesh, in all the languages of the ancient Mediterranean, the graffiti of the admiring visitors who, for more than one and a half thousand years, went to visit it.

Unperturbed by the attention lavished upon them, and unmoved by the tributes of mortals, they still stand, for all the world as if they were the fanatical guardians of the eternal Egypt. Their mutilated and blind faces stare eternally out over the desert, and, beyond it, at the sky of their kings and their gods.

Above: The temple of Luxor, in the midst of which a mosque has been erected. Seen along the right side: the Ramses II Obelisk. Upper right: the temple of Queen Hatshepsut in Thebes. Below: the Memnon colossi.

THE WAILING WALL

Since the 13th century BC the site of Jerusalem, known as Ophel Hill, had been occupied by a Caanean (?) and pagan people, the Jebusians. David conquered it around the year 1000 and built his palace there, as a home for the Ark of the Covenant—a wooden chest containing the tables of the law which had been given to Moses. He thus elevated the new city to the status of spiritual capital of the twelve unified Jewish tribes.

Solomon, his son and successor, who reigned from 972 to 932, undertook the construction of a gigantic and sumptuous palace while he was at the height of his power: the House of Yahve, and the heart of the Hebrew people. It was an ambitious venture, on a grand scale, which mobilized 150,000 workers from 966 to 959; it was made possible by the assistance of King Hiram of Tyr, who supplied materials, architects and craftsmen. Nothing precise is known about its layout and appearance, only that it stood on the rock where, according to the Bible, Abraham's sacrifice took place.

After resisting the first onslaught by the Assyrians under Sennacherib, in 701, Jerusalem was taken in 597 by Nebuchadnezzar, who destroyed its temple and deported most of its ablebodied inhabitants to Mesopotamia. Once Cyrus had become the master of Babylon he freed the Jews, in 538: Jerusalem was repopulated and a second temple, smaller and less richly endowed

than the first, was built on the same site (520-515). In 178 it in turn was sacked by Antiochos—one of Alexander's successors—who desecrated it by building a statue of Olympian Zeus in it.

Although he was a vassal of Rome, Herod, who was governor of the city in 48, started the construction of a third temple. He enlarged its foundations by building a huge platform of megalithic blocks, the north-west corner of which was defended by the Antonia citadel.

He then had the sanctuary built on this gigantic podium, over the rock of Abraham. A stout defensive wall surrounded all these cultural buildings within an enormous sacred enclosure, the Haram, an irregular rectangle whose sides vary from 300 to 500 feet.

Inside this first rampart the Courtyard of the Gentiles was open to non-Jews. It was here that the small-scale merchants who derived their livelihood from the crowds of pilgrims tended to congregate. A second courtyard was reserved for the Jews, and was named accordingly. It served as an ante-chamber to the sanctuary, which was divided into two areas, for men and women; on the other hand, the Holy of Holies, containing the sacred texts and the rock, was accessible only to the High Priest, once each year.

It was this set of buildings which was finally razed by Titus when he took Jerusalem (in 70 AD), expelling its inhabitants, who took refuge along the shores of the Dead Sea and then at Massada.

The Wailing Wall is what remains of the

western foundations of Herod's temple. It owes its name to the tears shed by the Jews with Jeremiah after the destruction of their sanctuary. Since then, this soldly built wall 500 feet long and 50 high, made of carefully assembled limestone blocks, has remained the symbol of the perennity of the Jewish people, throughout the changing fortunes of their history.

In itself it is a sort of Promised Land all of its own, an unattainable dream which was eventually realized when it was annexed by the State of Israel in 1967, after the Six Days' War, together with the Jordanian part of Jerusalem.

Israeli Jews go there for religious ceremonies and private celebrations or simply for a moment's quiet reflection before an important decision. The Jews of the Diaspora have made it their supreme ambition to stand and pray at the wall at least once in their lifetime. For this reason there is always a varied and colorful crowd in front of the wall: 'Sabras' mixed with soldiers, pilgrims and bearded Hassidim, with their broad black hats and plaited ringlets.

For them the Wailing Wall is a witness to their history and a living thing — virtually a being to whom they can confide their misfortunes and joys, a symbol of hope and at the same time a comfort. It has ceased to be inanimate: an Israeli refrain says that "unlike men with hearts of stone, it is made of stones with the hearts of men".

Jerusalem. The Wailing Wall of the Jews, with the faithful engaged in traditional lament and prayer.

THE DOME OF THE ROCK

In 638, six years after the death of Mohammed, the siege of Jerusalem by the Arabs of the new triumphant Islam had led to the virtually bloodless seizure of the town. The old city, which had already seen so much bloodshed, had chosen to open its doors to the great Omar, the second Ommayad Caliph. His first act on entering Jerusalem was to go to the ancient terrace of the temple of Solomon and Herod for a moment of recollection on the sacred rock, which he later had covered with a modest first Muslim sanctuary made of ornate wood.

unusual use of yellow and ochre tones illuminates the structure and enhances the sense of lightness and unreality conveyed by the splendid gilded cupola, the work of Hindu artisans in the 14th century. The resemblance between the sanctuary's silhouette and that of a Byzantine basilica is further heightened by the absence of minarets.

The fact that each caliph and sultan, in keeping with tradition, sought to list his name and acts of generosity accounts for the elegant frieze in Kufic script which runs around the outside of the building. The last inscription, which relates to Sultan Mahamud, dates from 831.

Four doors of carved wood lead into the

Several years later, in the midst of the great outburst of Arab power which took place in the 7th century, the new Caliph of Damascus, Abd-el-Malik, for a mixture of political and religious reasons, built one of the most beautiful structures of Islam, the *Qoubet-es-Sakhra,* or Dome of the Rock, on the same spot. Henceforth Jerusalem, the third of the Muslim holy places, began to rival Mecca and Medina. Large numbers of pilgrims came to the famous rock, the heart of the Semitic religions, which was venerated in both the Koran and the Bible, and which has numerous sacred associations: this was where Abraham came close to sacrificing his son Isaac, Mohammed ascended into heaven, Jacob's ladder linked heaven to earth, and Noah was thought to have moored his ark.

The Dome of the Rock, which was built in honor of Omar, was completed in 4 years (687-91) by regional architects and craftsmen, not all of whom were Muslim; this fact accounts for the Hellenic and Byzantine influences with which the building is imbued. Rather than the customary layout of the classical mosque, the sanctuary reminds us more of an ancient Roman mausoleum or an orthodox church.

It consists of an octagonal base, with 36 lattice-work windows, on which there is a slender drum supporting a dome which is both powerful and light, solid and harmonious. The outer face of the octagonal plinth is clad in superb Iranian glazed green and blue ceramics, offered by the Turkish Sultan Suleiman the Magnificent in 1545, to replace the original 7th-century enameled bricks. The same is true of the drum, where the

interior; they are situated at the cardinal points facing the stairs and are covered with bronze plaques. They also date from the time of Suleiman (16th century).

The mosque, the layout of which is circular, consists of two concentric aisles bordered by ancient columns, marbles, porticoes and capitals taken from famous ruins. If one adds to this the "stained glass" of the 16th century, some remains of 7th-century mosaics, Persian or Turkish carpets and a host of Iranian ceramics, one can see the extent to which this sanctuary is truly a museum of the civilizations of the Middle East.

The center of it all is the famous rock, through which a hole was once made and which has a central cavern of uncertain purpose. Some sources regard it as a secret hiding-place for hay and farm tools, while others believe it must have been a drain for the blood of sacrificed animals. This is the famous rock which the Archangel Gabriel (Djebraïl) prevented from rising into heaven after Mohammed.

After serving for a while as a Christian church, during the brief existence of the Christian kingdom of Jerusalem, it was restored to Islam by Saladin in 1287.

The Omar Mosque in Jerusalem, also known as the "Basilica of the Mount". Views of the parvis and from same. Cose-up glimpse of the mosaics.

royal banquet. This was the grandest royal building of the day: an immense hall 245 feet long bordered by 36 gigantic columns supporting on their amazing double-headed capitals (lions, horses or fabulous birds) a cedar platform over 60 feet high. It was here that the king used to hold his public audiences. The monumental stairway leading to it was covered with remarkable low reliefs which depicted in minute detail each of the provincial delegations taking part in the procession and the local products which they had brought: precious vases, rich fabrics, bracelets and jewels, ivory and gold and silver table-ware, chariots and even the cattle peculiar to each region, from the rams of Caria and the humped cows of the Caspian to Scythian horses and Bactrian camels.

Wherever one turned one saw symbols, on palace plinths and doorway lintels: rows of Medic or Persian warriors, the famous "immortals" which were thought to be the depositaries of armed force and guardians of the empire; images of the sovereign on his throne borne by representatives of the 14 nations of the empire; the king fighting Arhiman, the spirit of evil in Persian religion, shown with the features of a monstrous animal with forked clogs.

It was this superb and opulent city that Alexander found early in the winter of 311. And it was this masterpiece that he burned to the ground. It has been argued that he did so accidentally, after a night of drunken revelry; some claim that the burning was deliberate, as revenge for the desecration and burning of the temple of Athena on the Acropolis, some years before, by Xerxes.

Two angles on the Persepolis ruins. Above: the remains of a giant statue to be found at the entrance to the Old City.

PERSEPOLIS

Set against the foothills of one of the barren mountain ranges which cut across the monotonous splendor of the Iranian plateau, the site of Persepolis is in itself starkly majestic.

It was chosen to accomodate the new capital of the Achemenid empire which Darius sought to build; indeed he personally chose the site as a replacement for the noble city of Pansargade, which though historic and venerable, had become too small.

The new king needed to display the power and wealth of his empire for all the world to see, in order to strengthen the allegiance of its component nations and discourage all thought of secession.

This principle of domination through prestige, later borrowed by colonial Rome, accounts for the architecture of the buildings situated on the terrace at Persepolis. They are the expression of a State-inspired monumental art imbued with the notion of monarchy and designed to fulfil both political and esthetic purposes.

Their sumptuous nature and gigantic scale were intended to impress the delegates from the far-off provinces who had come to renew their submission to the king. They were constantly reminded of the divine essence of the dynasty by the images of Ahura Mazda, the winged god, which were to be seen on all the monumental structures at Persepolis.

Only the noblest of materials—marble, cedar, precious metals—were used. However, as a symbol of federalism, specialized craftsmen from all the provinces of the country were brought to work on the site: brickmakers from Babylon, stone-carvers from Egypt, Phenican carpenters, Syrian masons, Carian goldsmiths, etc.

Construction went on from 518 to 512, and kept more than a thousand workers permanently busy. Even so, when Darius died in 485 only the first segment of buildings had been completed, and Xerxes had to further enlarge and embellish the complex of the sacred terrace for another twenty years before giving it its final form.

Nothing in the ancient world had been so colossal, so grandiose or so sumptuous. Yet it was used only once a year, for the *Now-Roz,* the Iranian New Year, the day when the procession of dignitaries and delegates from the imperial provinces took place. Being a purely political and sacred capital city, Persepolis was not inhabited: the king and his court, as well as the national delegations, went there only for the duration of the ceremonies.

The enormous platform of massive stone blocks—the "terrace"—on which the processions took place covered over 32 acres and towered over the plain from a height of some 40 feet. This enormous podium could be reached by a double stairway with 111 steps. Once they had reached the top, the route followed by the delegations—and, until recently, by crowds of tourists—was invariable:

The monumental Gate of Xerxes flanked by two human-headed panels in the Assyrian style; the hall (9,500 sq. ft.) with a hundred columns, which served as Xerxes' throne room; the "treasury", which had been enlarged from the original throne room of Darius to form a maze of storage rooms in which the wealth paid in taxes by each province accumulated; the palace of Darius, and then of Xerxes, where the king gave an annual banquet for his nobles and the dignitaries of the empire; and lastly the Apadana, its stairs decorated with the carved figures of long rows of servants carrying lambs and jars to the

ISFAHAN

Isfahan, the prestigious capital of the fabulous Persia of the 17th century, owes its permanent prosperity to a remarkable location: in the center of the country, at an altitude of 5,000 feet, at the edge of the desert, yet watered unfailingly by an abundant river whose source is in the nearby Zagros mountains. For centuries past it has displayed in an enormous oasis-like plain the crown of its opulent gardens and orchards; they are surrounded by slender walls of baked mud on which it is still possible to see the lattice-work towers of the countless dovecotes which once supplied fertilizer for the crops. Isfahan became Islamic in 643 but was devastated by the invasions of the Mongols (1228) and Tamerlane (1388); it was not until 1598, when Shah-Abbas chose it as the capital of his empire, that the

period of its glory began.

Thereafter, for more than a century, it was embellished with the prodigious buildings and monuments for which it has since been famous—a testimony to the golden age of the civilization and art of the Sefevids.

The Royal Square was the center of this imposing city, which Shah-Abbas intended to symbolize the radiant power of a legendary Persia. Each side of the square is still occupied by an exceptional building from that opulent period.

To the north is the great gate of the main trading gallery, adorned with glazed ceramics and frescoes depicting banquets and battles. It is still possible to see the balconies on which the musicians used to play each evening at sunset, in honor of the glory of their king and of eternal Persia. To the east is the exquisite mosque of Sheikh Lotfollah (director of the theological

schools, or *medressee,* of the town). This building, which was completed in 1618, is remarkable for the exuberant perfection of its enameled cladding, and for the original, slightly flattened form of its dome, the principal colors of which—pastel, pink and cream—are also unusual in Islam. Being a private mosque intended for the king and his court, it has no minarets.

To the west is Ali Qapou, a Timurid pavilion which existed as early as the 15th century. Shah-Abbas added a spectacular royal loggia of ornate wood from which he, together with the court and his foreign guests, watched polo matches, displays and performances, as well as executions on the square below.

The Royal Mosque is interesting less for its classical layout than for its exceptionally rich and perfect decoration. All surfaces, whether flat or curved, domes or walls—are clad in a teeming

abundance of floral and geometrical patterns.

Despite this lavish polychrome display, which has a fairytale quality about it, the structure as a whole is a masterpiece of refined elegance and harmony.

Its contours and volume, which are both sober and majestic, are so well proportioned that this explosion of brilliant yet soft colors does not seem at all out of place.

The remarkable thing about this building is that it reconciles a gigantic architectural scale, the privacy needed for prayer and recollection, and the tumultuous florid brilliance of its decoration, which was intended to remind the faithful of the Garden of Allah.

Isfahan. Left: a minaret, with the dome and one of the archways through which one gains entrance to the *Medressa.* Above: the *Masdjed-i-Chah.*

HAGIA SOPHIA

At the end of the third century, the Roman emperors, troubled by Italian decadence, began to consider moving their capital eastwards, to the healthiest part of the empire. It was Constantine who chose, in 324, the site of the future Byzantium (Constantinople), on the western shores of the Bosphorus, on a neck of land bathed by the waters of the Golden Horn and the Sea of Marmara.

For almost ten years 40,000 workers toiled away building the new capital, the heart of which was inaugurated in 330. Columns and capitals were brought in from all over the Middle East to enhance its beauty. In order to give it a population, thousands of slaves were freed from bondage and large numbers of prisoners were released. Roman notables were induced to administer it by offers of superb new palaces.

From 505 onwards the emperor and his government resided there permanently. Originally Byzantium had very much the air of a transferred capital, as it was still wholly Roman. But very soon, under the influence of Hellenism and the Orient, it became cosmopolitan—a point of contact between Europe and Asia, the Mediterranean and Oriental worlds.

With more than a million inhabitants

Istanbul. The Saint Sophia Basilica: seen from within and without. Above: the *mirhab*.

Blue Mosque of Sultan Ahmed), the Hippodrome, and above all, Hagia Sophia, whose name in ancient Greek meant Holy Wisdom.

This towering and majestic shape, both massive and elegant, which dwarfed the other structures of the city, was the work of Justinian. He built it in 537 on the site of the former sanctuaries of Constantine and Theodosius. He wanted it to be "the most beautiful building in Creation". And, on the day it was consecrated, after delirious celebrations which had lasted several days, he had proudly exclaimed, when viewing his work: "Solomon, I have done better than you".

It was certainly the most sumptuous and grandiose piece of Christian architecture—and one which for more than nine centuries sent its radiance all over the Byzantine world. On a concrete base 20 feet thick, ten thousand workers under the command of a hundred foremen, had built this gem of stone and marble which stands 250 ft. high and 230 ft. wide.

40 columns which had been shipped from Egypt, Ephesus and Baaleck formed the outlines of a prodigiously slender nave, and supported a cupola whose dimensions made it unique in history: 180 ft. high and 100 ft. in diameter.

However, shaken by earthquakes which repeated earthquakes and made it essential to thicken the walls and consolidate the cupola, Hagia Sophia, which was turned into a mosque after the capture of Constantinople by the Otto-

under Justinian it eclipsed Rome, which had fallen to the Barbarians, and represented the heart of the new Eastern Christianity, with its flourishing art and civilization.

The centre of the city was the huge Augustan Forum, around which stood the principal public buildings: the Senate, the Augusteon, the Imperial Palace (on the site of the present

mans in 1453, gradually assumed its present contours. Now it is heavy and ponderous, stifled by irrelevant structures tacked onto it over the ages; from the outside a great deal of imagination is needed to visualize the radiant magnificence which it once had at the time of its splendor.

It is only on the inside that one can still appreciate its admirable majesty.

MECCA

Since 630, when Mohammed returned to his native town, Mecca has been the heart and the soul of the Muslim world.

In the pre-Islamic period it had been a mere hamlet deriving its livelihood from the Bedouin caravan trade across the Arabian Desert. The notables of Mecca formed a closed world of rich merchants who belonged for the most part to Jewish tribes which had settled in the Hedjaz, along the Red Sea coast.

There was already, in the center of the small town, a strange cube draped in black, the Kaaba, where worshippers venerated large numbers (more than 200!) of pagan idols, including a sun god, a god of love and a certain Allah.

In 570 Mohammed was born in Mecca in a family of merchants. It was not until he reached the age of 40 that he received the revelation of a new monotheistic religion adoring Allah, the sole and universal God.

His preaching quickly upset the conservative Jewish merchants, and he had to flee to Medina in 622. His exile constitutes the *Hegira,* or starting point of the Muslim calendar and of the conquests of Islam. After years of struggling, preaching and meditation, in which the substance of the Koran was revealed to them, Mohammed's followers seized Mecca, which promptly submitted to the new spiritual power (622). In 630 the Prophet, who had smashed the idols of the Kaaba and denounced paganism, proclaimed the universal and absolute reign of Allah.

The progress of Mohammed's cause was not, however, entirely smooth. In 930 the Black Stone was stolen by the extremist Shiites known as the Karmathians who returned it only 8 years later, against a ransom; the holy places were occupied by the Mamelukes of Egypt and then by the Ottomans (1517); the Sherifs of Mecca made an attempt to secede, and were driven out by King Ibn Seoud at the beginning of the century.

Yet Mecca is still irresistibly fascinating for Muslims, whose supreme ambition is to go there at least once as a pilgrim.

Every year a million pilgrims come to this desert town, which lies at the foot of a rocky *djebel.* Great changes have had to be made in order to receive them: modern boulevards have been laid out, with huge parking lots to accommodate the cars which have replaced the camels of old; gigantic hotels have sprouted from the sand to house the travelers, instead of the nomads' tents which once enlivened the desert landscape. Yet the fervor is the same, despite the brisk and voracious business done by the parasitic entertainers and salesmen, who are not unlike those to be found at all the world's major centers of pilgrimage.

The town itself and its vicinity are sacred and are out of bounds to non-Muslims. In fact the holy of holies is the Haram-al-Sharif, an immense circular mosque shaped like a crown, with tall minarets towering above it. Its façade, which has recently been cleared of the urban clutter which had stifled it for centuries has numerous gateways, through which the steady stream of visitors can pass easily.

Inside this circular mosque is a colossal courtyard, surrounded by a series of delicate arcades with small bare domes. The starkness of the place is enhanced by the sobriety and austerity of the buildings, which have no ornaments or signs of superfluous opulence. In the midst of this open area, through which the pilgrims can move about freely, is the Kaaba.

According to tradition, it was built by Adam or Seth, destroyed by the Flood and rebuilt by Abraham with the help of his son Ishmael.

The Black Stone, which is built into one corner, was given by the Archangel Gabriel (Djebrail). It is a cube 48 feet high and 38 feet wide which has, for several centuries, been draped in a cover of black brocade, the *kiswa,* around the edges of which a series of verses from the Koran is embroidered in gold thread. Every year a new *kiswa,* made in Egypt, is brought to Mecca and installed in the midst of much ceremony.

Travelers arriving in Mecca to perform their pilgrimage *(Hajj)* are obliged to follow an unchanging ritual: they have to be shaved and put on a white cloth robe before entering the *haram.* Then they must kiss the Black Stone (doubtless a meteorite), and at least touch the Kaaba before walking around the building seven times *(tawaf);* then follows the ascent to the top of Mount Arafat, where the Koran was revealed to Mohammed; after which they go to Mina, to throw stones at three columns, in memory of Abraham stoning the devil.

These rites take up a total of twelve days. For obvious reasons of climate the official pilgrimage takes place in winter, though pilgrims are free to go when they like. In days gone by the journey itself was so long and perilous that it was an actual part of the pilgrimage, and the numerous travelers who died on the sun-baked trails of the Hedjaz were, just like those engaged in the Hajj of today, entitled to the eternal indulgence of Allah. For men of whatever standing in life, for Muslims and Christians alike, the name of Mecca is laden with strange and fascinating associations.

Among the shifting sands and roasted rocks of Arabia there doubtless lies an exalting trace of one of the greatest upsurges of mystical feelings ever to have thrilled the human soul.

The Great Mosque at Mecca, with its minarets and, centrally featured, the *Kaaba.*

THE PARTHENON

The imposing hulk of what was once the most beautiful temple in the city of Pericles still towers over Athens from the top of the Acropolis, a venerable rocky outcrop which bears numerous archeological scars. Whereas the Agora was the center of Athenian public life, the Acropolis was its sacred district, which was reached by a monumental set of stairways and porticoes which made up the *Propylea*. On the rocky plateau, which has been splendidly rounded and carved by many centuries of erosion, and which was once filled with statues and votive offerings, the following ruins are still to be seen:

The Temple of Athena Nike, as one enters the Acropolis, an elegant and distinguished structure, though somewhat cold. Further on, the Erectheion, with its world-famous but ailing Cariatids. And, above all, the poignant and breathtaking ruins of the Parthenon, which confronts the visitor head-on, its platform standing at the same

height as the pediments of the Propylea.

Dedicated to Athena Parthenos—the Virgin—and not to Minerva, it succeeded two rudimentary earlier temples built under Pisitrates on the same site, which had been destroyed by fire. The second had been deliberately burnt, sacked and desecrated by the Persian Xerxes in May 480, after the disaster at Thermopylae. The third temple, whose ruins we admire today, was built between 447 and 432 during the rule of Pericles, at the highest point of Athenian art and civilization.

It was of an atypical Doric order, in the sense that it had eight columns across its façade instead of six, and seventeen on each side.

Hewn from the purest white Pentelican marble, its columns, which are more than 39 ft. high, were fluted on the site itself in order to avoid damage during transport. The brilliant Phidias was in charge of construction: he chose as architect Ictionos, who had already built the temple of Bassae, at a superbly isolated spot on a hilltop in the Peloponnese.

Actually the Parthenon, which rested on a massive platform of limestone blocks, is of relatively modest proportions (228 ft. by 98). An ingenious technical ploy was used, however, to make it look bigger: through the use of slight curves in each straight segment of stone, and by having the columns converge gently inwards, it had been given a barely perceptible convexity which added an unusual degree of softness to the "magnified" contours thus produced. This original design also enabled it to better withstand the earthquakes which are common in the region.

On the inside it has two parts:

The Cella, which contained a giant marble and ivory statue of Athena, more than 35 feet tall, made by Philias; and the Virgins' Room, where the goddess's offerings and treasures were stored. The public funds of the city were also kept here. Indeed one is tempted to think that the Parthenon was really a huge sacred treasury and a symbol of

the power of Athens, the role of sanctuary of Athena belonging in fact to the Erectheion.

The sumptuous quality of the decorative work and of the materials used (a superb cedar roof and a marble paneled ceiling) enhanced the powerful majesty of the building's lines by adding a refined gracefulness.

What really made the Parthenon unique was the perfection of the sculptures with which it was abundantly adorned. Its two pediments, in particular, were fully occupied by magnificent low reliefs depicting, in the east, the birth of Athena and, in the west, the divine conflict between Athena and Poseidon.

Yet the gem of this exceptional decoration was the broad and admirable sculpted frieze covering the top of the outer walls of the temple and known by the name *Panathenea*.

It immortalized in stone the great festivals held each summer in Athens, at which a succession of competitions involving music, poetry and sport took place. In particular, a long procession went from the Agora to the Acropolis to carry a new *peplos* to the statue of Athena on the Erectheion. Phidias had carved a detailed record of the ceremony, in the form of two long processional rows which met above the entrance to the temple. Like all the buildings of antiquity, the Parthenon was painted, in accordance with an unchanging ritual, with broad stripes of blue, red and gold. The statues themselves were enhanced with gold and bronze plaques.

Athens. Assorted views of the Acropolis.

The city of Delphi is certainly worthy of the god Apollo, its creator: it is situated in a superb natural amphitheater at the foot of Mount Parnassus, near the north shore of the Gulf of Corinth, from which it is separated by the sea of ancient olive trees of the Bay of Itea.

Originally, during the Mycenian period (12th century BC) it was only a small fertility sanctuary dedicated to the earth goddess, Ge. Its glory and wealth came in the 8th century, when Apollo went there to vanquish the monstrous python, making it a shrine in his own honor.

The small city of Phocides, where a population of a thousand people lived on the business brought by pilgrims, declared itself independent, thus giving rise to several sacred wars, as the Phocidians sought to recover their town and, above all, its treasures.

After a period of changing fortunes, and the destruction of the first two temples (548 and 373) by fire and earthquake, Delphi came under the administration of the twelve strongest Greek cities, which rebuilt the sanctuary whose ruins we now visit today (370 to 330).

Kings and notables all went to Delphi to consult the oracle before making an important decision, and then thanked it by leaving magnificent votive offerings, thus making this rocky patch of land richer than the most opulent metropolis of the fertile plains below.

The main part of the town was enclosed within a stout wall. A paved "sacred" road wound its way up to the temple of Apollo between rows of offerings which surpassed each other in their magnificence.

This road led to the megalithic platform on which stood the sanctuary of Pythian Apollo: a classic Doric temple, made of marble, with 6 columns along the façade and 15 on each side, and a basement containing two vaulted rooms devoted to the oracular utterances of the Pythia. Just uphill from the site is a remarkably well preserved theatre seating 5,000; the stadium at the top of the hill, which has seating for 7,000 spectators, was the setting for the Pythian games which started in 590 and were held once every four years, between the Olympiads. The famous Castalian fountain still flows from the mouth of a narrow gorge, just below the sanctuary, at the place where, according to legend, the fight between the Python and the god took place; it is situated at the foot of the Phedriades Gorges, from which condemned men—the most famous of whom was Aesop—used to be thrown.

Delphi was not a town but a sanctuary in the custody of two priests who were appointed for life, a number of "prophets" and a host of servants of the divine cult. The oracle pronounced by the Pythia was its greatest glory.

Originally, young girls were used, but it was not long before women of over 50 were brought into service. Moreover, the early practice of three oracular utterances each year was changed in response to heavy demand, so that three of them were permanently on duty and had to perform their rites several times a month.

The fascination of Delphi lies in the exceptional and highly evocative mystical atmosphere which still pervades its ruins, laid out on the mountainside.

This celebrated ancient site is a perfect example of total harmony between the rugged and random shapes of raw nature and the majestic product of man's search for divinity.

The ruins at Delphi couched in their awesome surroundings.

THE ALHAMBRA

In the fifth century BC Granada was a tiny out-of-the-way hamlet; though it did become a moderately large Roman settlement some 800 years later, it returned to the status of insignificant village (*granata,* whence its name), on the Cerro del Sol, by the late Middle Ages. Its glorious history did not really begin until the coming of the Arabs. Having been invaded, like the whole of the rest of Andalusia, in the eighth century, it rose to prominence after the decline of the Ommayad caliphates of Seville and Cordoba, and, in the 12th century, became an independent kingdom under the control of the Almohad sultans of Moroccan origin.

The Alhambra dates from this privileged period. This magnificent fortified palace, which is famous the world over, was the gem of its day. The citadel, which girdles the hill with its tall fawn walls (*Alhambra* means 'the red' in Arabic) seems to form an immense crenellated crown, high above the city. The outer wall of rust-colored bricks, has many gates and fortified towers throughout its total length of more than 700 yards. It once served to protect a closed world of palaces and gardens in which the Muslim princes had sought to reproduce the atmosphere of scented and subdued refinement, to the sound of gently splashing fountains, which was dear to their hearts.

The oldest part of the Alhambra is the private rooms of Yussuf I (the Comares and Myrtle Towers), while the rest is the work of his son Mohammed V (14th century).

Throughout the entire palace, however, one is treated to the same festival of monumental Arab art, which here reaches its highest levels of refinement: finely chiseled and sculpted stucco frescoes; exquisite inlaid cedar and spruce panels; superb stalactite ceilings and pendants highlighted in gold; elegant columns and rare and

precious marbles, light and delicate cupolas.

The pinnacle of this Islamic art in Spain is the Courtyard of the Lions, designed in 1377. In a small area, measuring only 100 ft by 50, it embodies the quintessence of the elegance and the charm of this Moorish civilization: 124 graceful and delicate columns, 20 ft tall, produce the wondrous and unreal setting for a tale from the Thousand and One Nights.

In the middle is the famous fountain, consisting of 12 roughly sculpted lions, which is something of an anomaly in the annals of Islamic art, as the Koran forbids human and animal images.

Another remarkable element of this refined comfort, which was exceptional for its period and quite unknown in the European Middle Ages, is the baths of Yussuf I, a haven of cool, scented peace, away from the world.

Besides which there is the extraordinary view, from each gallery, of the Granada hills, which lie baking in the sun; the distant sounds of the real world rise vaguely through the hot air towards this paradise, tucked away behind its reddish walls.

It is easy to understand the despair of Boadil, the last Moorish master of Granada, who was obliged to flee his enchanted hilltop by a gate which has since remained closed. He looked back sadly to take one last glance at his other-wordly palace, from a mountain pass which has since been known as The Sigh of the Moor.

The Alhambra in Granada. An overall view, the gardens, and the Court of Lions.

THE ESCORIAL

The imposing and austere mass of the Monastery of San Lorenzo, better known by the name of the small nearby hamlet, El Escorial, stands on the stark and arid slopes of the Sierra de Guadarrama, 30 miles from Madrid.

It is a palace-cum-monastery, built by Philip II, in memory of his father Charles V, and also in fulfilment of a vow.

Everything is on a monumental scale: 16 courtyards, 860 stairways, 300 rooms, more than 1,200 doors and 2,500 windows, within the perfect and sharply delineated rectangles of 690 ft by 530 which encompasses the building.

The Escorial contains no fewer than 3 churches and 15 cloisters—evidence of the religious mania which tormented Philip II in his declining years. On the other hand, the 88 fountains and the delightful gardens with their ornamental ponds temper this monastic austerity by providing a discreet reminder of the charms of the Moorish palaces in reconquered Andalusia.

The core of the building is its huge central courtyard (210 ft by 125 ft) the Patio de Los Reyes. The church, the spiritual center of the palace, stands with its clifflike exterior, stands at one end. It fits nicely into the generally gigantic scale of the place: its façade is propped up by six stout columns supporting bronze statues of the kings of Judah, and by the two imposing towers which look down over the granite forecourt from a height of 300 ft.

The Pantheon of the kings of Spain, a crypt adorned with black marble, below the main chapel, containing 26 grey sarcophagi, is also in harmony with the atmosphere of cold rigor which pervades the entire place.

However, the successors of Philip II, lacking his fondness for monastic asceticism, piled up a profusion of fabulous treasures after his death: paintings by the Great Masters of the period, a Christ by Benvenuto Cellini, and many rare and precious objects.

The sacristy, the chapter room of the smaller cloister and the library are genuine museums. The labyrinthine 'palace' consists of a tangle of chambers and ante-chambers packed with furniture, paintings and objects whose value is matched only by their variety.

El Escorial seen from three vantage points.

LA GIRALDA

Seville, the ancient Hispalis, was successively the prey of the Phenicians, the Carthaginians, the Greeks and the Romans until the eighth century. Its destiny changed when, in 710, mounted Moroccan Berbers were sent by the Arabs to reconnoiter Andalusia. Doubtless pleased with their first impressions, they landed on the orders of Tarik in 711, on a large rocky headland which was promptly named *Djebel Tarik* (modern Gibraltar) and then along the coast. They met scarcely any resistance and, showing respect for the property of the peasants, they refrained from looting. Within the year Andalusia was conquered. Musa himself participated in the Arab invasion with his son Abd-el-Aziz, who in 712 was made governor of the new Islamic province of Spain, under the suzerainty of the Omayad Caliphs of Damascus. Abd-el-Aziz chose Seville as his capital.

For five centuries, this rival of Cordoba and Granada became impregnated with Arab culture and civilization and was embellished with some superb Islamic architecture. In fact, despite the 'reconquest' of the city in 1248 by Ferdinand III, who restored it to Christendom, its scent of jasmine and its fondness for glazed ceramic tiles *(azulejos)* still serve as a nostalgic reminder of the splendors of its Muslim past.

Without realizing it perhaps, the conquerors must have been moved by such feelings, because, although they demolished most of the Islamic buildings, for reasons of religious fanati-

cism, they could not bring themselves to do away with the most beautiful of them all: the Alcazar, the Golden Tower and the Giralda. Moreover, having promptly destroyed the mosque—too visible a symbol of a rival creed—they did not have the courage to pull down its superb minaret.

Better still, they completed it, in a sense annexing it to their own cult, adding a lantern, a clock, some bells, and, most prominently, a gigantic 19th-century bronze statue of Faith carrying a banner. It is so well balanced that it turns on its own axis, like a giant weathervane, at the slightest breath of wind; this phenomenon accounts for its present name, as *Giralda* derives from the Spanish verb *girar,* which means to turn. In 1420 a rather ponderous cathedral was built on the site of the razed mosque, with the result that La Giralda is attached to it.

La Giralda was built at the end of the 12th century on a square base (40 ft square) and, having very solid brick walls over eight ft thick, stands 230 ft tall. Inside there is a broad spiral ramp, including 28 landings, wide enough for two mounted men to ride side by side, which climbs to the upper terrace.

Sevilla. *La Giralda* with, above, the Plaza de España.

THE TOWER OF BELEM

According to tradition and legend, Ulysses founded Lisbon. In actual fact, *Ulisipo* was the name of a Phenician trading post which gave rise to the misunderstanding. The Roman settlement took over the same site, corresponding to the modern district of Alfama, the heart of the old town, on the right bank of the Tagus.

Portuguese expansion was linked to the growth of its maritime empire and the decisive role of the discoverer-prince, Henry the Navigator (1394-1460). From the rocky coast at Sagres, facing the ocean, he launched his ships on voyages of discovery along the major sea routes. Bartolomeu Dias, Vasco de Gama and Albuquerque, among others, sailed the seas and secured vast overseas territories—particularly Brazil—for the Portuguese crown. They then set up new trade routes, in the quest for wheat, spices and the rich merchandise of Africa, the Far East and the Indies.

This saga of gallantry, seamanship and trading ability led to immense prosperity for Portugal. The rich merchants, leaving the noisy and crowded center of the city, moved to splendid mansions in what quickly became the upper-class district of Belém (a contraction of *Bethlehem*) on the right bank of the mouth of the Tagus.

King Manuel I (1495-1526), who did not share his predecessors' fondness for Bathala, built

in the new quarter the sumptuous monastery of the Jerónimos and the famous Tower of Belém.

Originally it was a fortress sitting on a rocky islet just offshore, where it was intended to defend the banks of the river and deny an enemy access to the city. Although it has now been joined to the mainland by silt deposits, it still retains its proud bearing.

Manuel I commissioned Francisco de Arruda to build the Tower. Having lived for a long time in Morocco, this brother of Diego, who had built Tomar, embodied in his work the full range of ornamental wealth of Manueline Baroque art, together with strong Moorish overtones. The result is a gem of elegance and power, blending classical Lusitanian severity and solidity with the teeming opulence of the Manueline Renaissance and the refined charm of the Islamic towers. Seeking to symbolize Portuguese maritime power, he chose to make the tower look like a ship's prow advancing along the river.

The overall impression is one of a defensive medieval fortress. But the fine quality of its ornamentation and stonework softens its military character so considerably that it becomes a masterpiece of ornate architecture.

The Belem Tower welcoming the visitor to Lisbon Port. Various glimpses of the Tage River and a close-up of the tower-face waterside.

27

COLOSSEUM

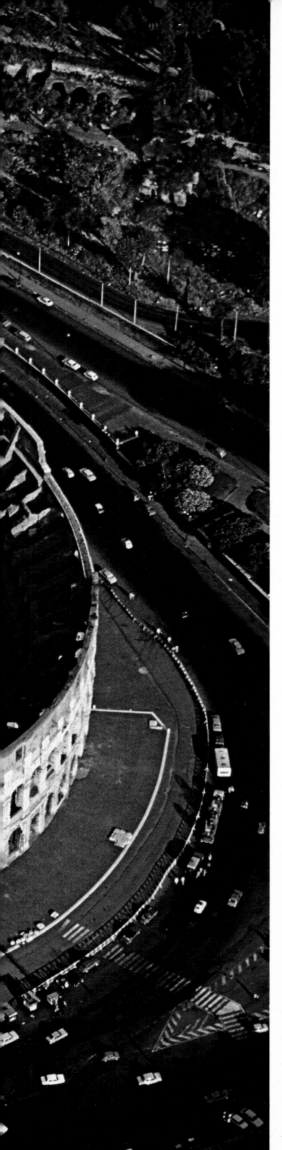

The Colosseum, which was inaugurated in the year 80 AD, was built over a period of eight years on a drained plot of land, in the former depression of Nero's Golden House, by Vespasian and Titus of the dynasty of the Flavians. It was completed by Domitian, the third Flavian, who added the third floor. Restored by Septimus Severus in 217, and in 445 after an earthquake, it remained intact until the time of Charlemagne, after which it began to deteriorate: it suffered two more earthquakes (1231 and 1255) and eventually came to be used as a quarry by the builders of the Farnese Palace and St. Peter's Basilica in the Vatican.

Its capacity has been variously estimated at between 50,000 and 80,000 spectators. Thanks to a very sensible layout of the stairs, the whole place could be filled and emptied quickly and safely. 175 ft high, 610 long and 500 wide, and built of travertine marble, it has 80 arcades which served as entrances. The principal one, being wider and taller than the rest, was reserved for the emperor.

The layout of the Colosseum is simple but grand; its functional architecture was embellished by a gallery above each set of tiers. The capitals were Doric, Ionic or Corinthian, depending on the floor. Today only the north-east section of wall is still standing, its original contours more or less clearly perceptible. Yet it is immediately evident that this must have been the most grandiose structure in the whole of ancient Rome. It is certainly the biggest of all Roman amphitheaters, surpassing those of El Djem and Nîmes.

As one stands before these eviscerated though still impressive ruins, a great effort of imagination is required in order to visualize the Colosseum in its prime: entirely white and bristling with marble colonnades supporting statues. 76 of the 80 entrances were open to the public, while the other four were reserved. In the middle was that of the emperor, crowned by a bronze quadriga; on either side, those of the gladiators, animals or prisoners and staff.

The seats of the privileged were shielded from the sun by broad *velatia,* held up by tall masts. The Cavea was divided, after all, into several bays, each assigned to a distinct social class: the notables lower down, the citizens in the middle and the proletariat at the top. From the top of these tiers the arena seemed even more immense, as did the *pulvinar,* or imperial platform situated in the front row on a huge podium. Nowadays the stone covering of this structure has disappeared, revealing the impressive skeleton of the foundation walls, where gladiators, con-demned prisoners and wild animals awaited the start of the day's show.

The games were held frequently and were often sumptuous. They were staged at the expense of the emperor or the dignitaries and fulfilled an unmistakable political purpose, *panem et circenses* being a cynical philosophy of government at the time. The games, to which admission was free, were a right, not a luxury. Actually the Romans loved this savage and brutal form of combat which, like the Spanish bullfight, was based on a fairly precise ritual.

Well before the opening of the games, the motley crowd spread over the marble tiers, sitting on cushions sold by vendors; it was quite common to eat there too.

The games then began, with the *editor* serving as a kind of master of ceremonies: after the entry of the gladiators, to tumultuous applause, and their famous "Hail, Caesar, those who are about to die salute thee", they pitted against each other a variety of combatants, each with a distinctive weapon—net, trident or sabre—until a similarly ritual death, accompanied by the "thrumbs-down" sign, the *police verso,* on the part of the emperor.

Rome. Three views of the Coliseum.

ST PETER'S, ROME

Whereas the tiny Vatican City (110 acres) came into being as late as 1929, on the signing of the Lateran Treaty, St Peter's Basilica, which is widely regarded as the wonder of Rome, has existed in its present condition since 1626. Its setting is quite remarkable: at the end of the extraordinary elliptical St Peter's Square, one of the finest in the world and, measuring as it does 1,100 ft by 780 ft, one of the largest. It was built in 10 years (1657 to 1667) by Bernino, who surrounded it with a quadruple colonnade (284 columns 65 ft tall) supporting a balustrade bearing 140 evenly spaced statues of the saints (nearly 13 ft tall).

This exceptional architectural complex makes a grand and impressive introduction to the most famous basilica in the Christian world. A ramp and a staircase, framed by two colossal statues of St Peter and St Paul, lead up to the basilica itself.

The site of the famous Nero's Circus, the center of which is occupied by Caligula's obelisk—traditionally held to be the place where Christians were martyred and St Peter buried—was the spot chosen by Constantine in 324 for the construction of a basilica which was to remain standing for more than 11 centuries. However, the year 1450, when Nicholas V decided to enlarge and alter it, marked the beginning of the building's incredible misfortunes: the pace of work was slow and hesitant; Michelangelo got the project moving in earnest, thereafter working on it until his death in 1564.

In its present state, the basilica covers an area of nearly 4 acres (three times the size of Notre Dame de Paris); its overall length exceeds 650 ft, and that of the transept 420 ft; the height of the nave is 150 ft. The dome, which has a diameter of 136 ft, reached its apex 370 ft above the ground.

The statistics, of course, do not alter two basic facts: the plan eventually used was more or less that intended by Michelangelo, and it is one of the grandest monuments in the world, and certainly the masterpiece of the Italian Renaissance and Baroque combined.

The interior creates an impression of grandiose and majestic serenity which, though tempered by the perfect harmony of proportions, is perhaps a little cold.

The most impressive aspct of St Peter's is, however, the fantastic dome, supported by four enormous pillars (230 ft in circumference).

Saint Peter's Basilica in Rome, with its pediment, the great dome, the nave, and the decorated interior of the dome.

THE LEANING TOWER OF PISA

First Greek, then Etruscan and finally Roman (180 BC), Pisa owed its medieval prosperity to its privileged geographical situation. In the center of a fertile Tuscan plain, 6 miles from the sea, its port on the Arno was the instrument of its mercantile expansion towards the east, and made it a rival for Genoa, Venice and Florence. Leonardo da Vinci even studied a project which would have diverted the Arno from its course, thus destroying the commercial potential of the port of Pisa.

During its period of opulence, the city was embellished by some superb buildings, which rank among the finest of the Italian Renaissance. The most famous of them are grouped together on the Piazza del Duomo, where they make a particularly fine and homogeneous spectacle.

The Leaning Tower, which, of all the structures on the Piazza, symbolizing Pisa's past glory, is most famous throughout the world.

The Tower is a typically Tuscan campanile, built in the Romanesque Pisan style by Bonnano Pisano, starting in 1174. It was a colossal venture, which took more than a century to finish. 14,000 tons of white marble went into this circular tower. It has 8 floors, with a total of 207 sculpted columns; its overall height is 180 ft and its circumference at the base is 155 ft.

The fact that it leans, however, is what has made it famous all over the world. It has been claimed by some that the architects intended it as a virtuouso demonstration of their ability to defy and overcome gravity.

In actual fact, however, it seems quite certain that the inclination is really accidental, as a number of churches in Pisa subsided at about the same time. Having been built on swampy, poorly drained land, near a number of underground springs, the building sank while it was being built, in fact when three floors had already been completed. After careful calculations the architects decided to press on anyway, while distinctly altering the design of the sides of the building. From 1275 onwards, one century after the laying of the first stone, corrections began to be made on the fourth floor: the columns on the leaning side were made perceptibly taller in order to gradually right the building and ensure that the terminal platform would be horizontal, as desired.

The results of their endeavors are actually surprising, as, despite numerous earthquakes over the years, the tower did not budge and seems to be structurally very sound indeed.

Its exterior decoration is reminiscent of the style of the Cathedral and the Baptistry: ample arcades, very 'florid', in the Pisan manner, with an emphasis on sumptuous effects and grandiose elegance which had a great influence throughout Tuscany.

Inside the tower, a spiral staircase with 292 steps leads to the small terrace from which Galileo conducted his experiments on gravitation and the properties of falling bodies.

From the top there is a magnificent view of the delightful Pisan landscape, the lush valley of the Arno and the superb buildings nearby.

THE PONTE VECCHIO

The River Arno is a kind of Florentine fetish. Like history itself, its irregular flow has always set the pace for the turbulent life of the ancient Tuscan city. The modern city, just like the opulent capital of the Medicis, lives and throbs on its banks. This veritable emblem of the Tuscan capital, a silhouette famous throughout the world and dear to the hearts of all Florentines, was built in the early 14th century.

Its two stout pillars support three arches across the river. To begin with, butchers' stalls ran the length of both sides of the bridge—doubtless a convenient location, as offal and scraps could easily be thrown over the side. The smell, however, could not have been very pleasant in summer, as Cosimo de Medicis I, Grand Duke of Tuscany, decided in the 16th century to move the butchers out and replace them with jewelry shops. The stalls were pulled down and the shops were arranged in two rows, overhanging the river so as not to make the roadway unduly narrow.

Not long afterwards, the same Cosimo I— not to be confused with Cosimo the Elder (1389-1464), the founder, 130 years earlier, of the signoria of the Medicis over the city—had the strange idea of linking his private residence in the Palazzo Pitti, on the left bank of the river, to the seat of government in the Palazzo Vecchio, on the right bank. This involved the construction of an astonishing covered gallery above the rows of small shops. Cosimo's architect, Vasari, took charge of the scheme. Part of this amazing suspended corridor can still be seen, above the shops on the eastern side of the bridge, and along part of the right bank as far as the beginning of the Palazzo della Signoria.

The Ponte Vecchio is an ideal place for visitors to stroll and relax, as the inhabitants of Florence pass by, against a superb medieval background. The site of the bridge was particularly well chosen: it is the most direct and the most heavily traveled route between the Oltrano district and the Palazzo Pitti, on the one hand, and the famous squares of the Palazzo Vecchio and the cathedral, which figure so prominently in the art and history of the Renaissance, on the other.

Left: the Leaning Tower of Pisa. Above: the Ponte Vecchio in Florence.

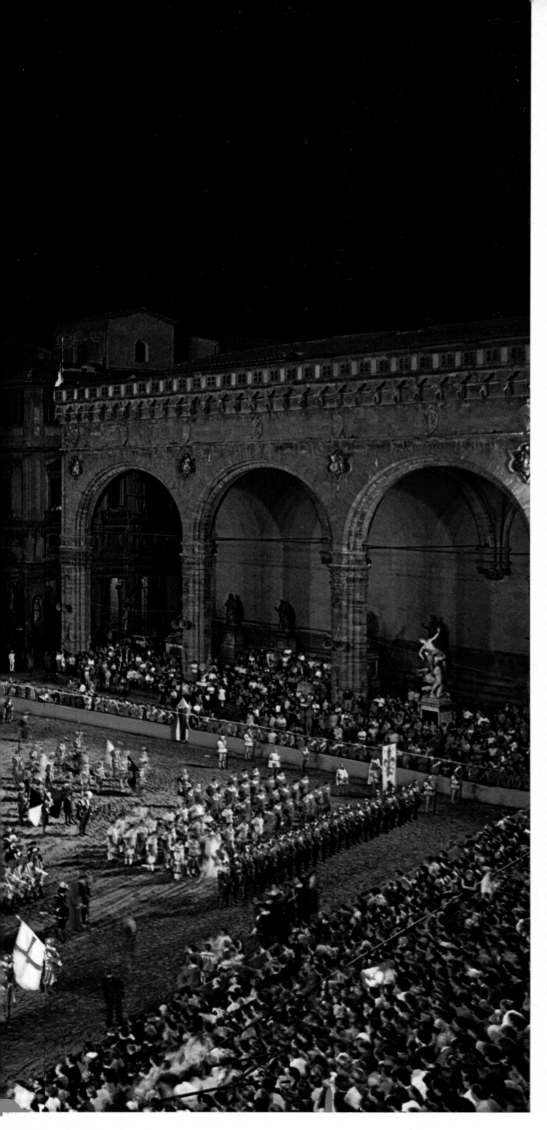

THE PALAZZO VECCHIO, FLORENCE

In the late Middle Ages, under Charlemagne, Florence was already a pleasant little town. But it foundered during the 12th century as a result of a succession of plots and domestic wars against rival cities in Central Italy. However, once these upheavals were over, it managed in 1267 to become an independent republic and to extend its authority over the whole of Tuscany. Prestige and opulence came with the advent of the Medici dynasty, the work of Cosme I, the 'Father of Florence', and the most perfect example of the 'signorias' which fragmented Italy between from the 13th to the 16th centuries.

Although they did not occupy any official office, Cosme I (1389-1494) and his descendants wielded total personal power by means of their influence in many spheres. Lorenzo the Magnificent (1448-1492) was to be the symbol of that omnipotence which, though open to challenge from the social and political points of view, had a highly beneficial effect on the arts and culture.

It is well to remember that they were the ones who made Florence the undisputed and influential cradle of the Italian Renaissance, the place where the brilliant ideas of the finest artists and craftsmen of the period matured before sweeping across the whole of Europe.

Florence, which is the most interesting city in Italy, together with Rome, has numerous monuments, museums and other buildings which testify to that that magnificence. Among them, the Palazzo Vecchio, or Palazzo della Signoria, is the richest and the most characteristic. This perfect example of civilian architecture at the time of the signorias stands on the small Piazza della Signoria, near where the Puritan monk Savanarola was burned to death, its powerful fawn-colored mass towering over the equestrian statue of the Cosme and a fountain in honor of Neptune.

It was begun in 1298 by Arnolfo de Cambio, and was chosen as his residence by Cosme de Medici in the 15th century. Having been the Italian Parliament building between 1865 and 1871, it is now the City Hall of Florence. This severe yet elegant building has a broad façade of rust-colored stone, above which there is a covered and crenellated sentry path. The majestic pediment is adorned with a row of four sculpted statues, including the *Lion of Florence* by Donatello, and Michelangelo's *David*. The graceful Arnolfo Tower, which rises above it to a height of 350 ft, is a fine transcription of the style of the religious campanile to secular architecture.

The palace is highly interesting because of the opulent decoration of its rooms and the wealth of the furniture which they contain. Wherever one looks—in the private rooms of Maria Salviati, the niece of Cosme I, in the drawing rooms and studies of Francisco de Medici on the first floor, or in the lavishly appointed rooms on the second floor which were used as a suite by the Medici family—one is treated to an abundance of paintings, ivory, enamel, porcelain and rare or precious objects which reflect the opulence as well as the good taste and the refinement of the Medici family. They also symbolize the cultural ferment of a period of profound civilization and radiant beauty.

Florence. The Palazzo Vecchio and the Loggia dei Lanzi.

SAINT MARK'S, VENICE

When the Barbarians invaded the rich plain of the Venetes in 450 AD, they forced the inhabitants to abandon their villages and seek refuge on the small islands at the sea's edge, near the mouth of the Po. Little by little, founding fishermen's hamlets as a way of surviving and later building more highly structured settlements, they brought into being the first Venetia, which elected its first Doge in 697. In 810 it was decided that the future capital, Venice, would be built on the island of Rivo.

Isolation and the surrounding sea, which had once provided the Venetes with security, were soon to make them rich. The resourceful, intelligent and adventurous Venetian merchants were the masters of the entire Mediterranean basin. Led by their Doge Dandolo (aged 94), they even took part in the seizure of Constantinople by the Crusaders in 1204, thus symbolically assuming the spiritual and commercial heritage of Byzantium in relations between East and West.

They thereby came into open conflict with Genoa for supremacy, which they finally secured after the Genovese defeat of 1380. Thereafter, for two centuries, the 14th and 15th, Venice was the undisputed master of trade in the eastern Medi-terranean. The already declining prestige of the venerable city, softened by high living and pleasures during the 16th and 17th centuries, was further damaged by the murderous raids of the triumphant Turks.

Their business contacts with Greece and Byzantium naturally led the Doges to turn to Greek artists and Byzantine influences when it was decided, in the 9th century, to build a monumental basilica to receive the body of Saint Mark, which had been brought from Alexandria in 823. Built between 829 and 832, Saint Mark's basilica is still the outstanding masterpiece of Venetian architecture, despite alterations carried

out between 1063 and 1971 and subsequent restorations in the 13th, 15th and 17th centuries.

Its architects drew their inspiration from Hagia Sophia, in Constantinople. Byzantine influence can be detected in its layout, based on the Greek cross and curiously covered with cupolas.

St.Mark's Square in Venice, with, in the background, the Cathedral. Left: throughway to the Grand Canal.

The interior is so lavishly decorated with mosaics and precious materials that the basilica has come to be known as the Golden Church *(Chiasa d'Oro).*

The façade is also richly laden with decorative detail, as its lower level consists of a colonnade embracing 5 portals and 5 arcades. The central portal is flanked by 4 marble columns and supports 11th-century bronze panels. The upper level is taken up by the famous and superb *quadriga* of horses made of gilded copper, an outstanding Greek masterpiece of the fourth century BC, which was 'recovered' at Constantinople in 1204.

In the penumbra which is only faintly illuminated by the sparse daylight filtering in from the cupolas, begins the dazzling, enchanting display of decorative lavishness and brilliance: several hundred columns, all made of pink marble, more than an acre of polychrome mosaics, and gold and silver inlays. It is both a museum and a magical treasure chest, laden with rare or precious objects. Saint Mark's is an artistic delight: in an area measuring 245 ft by 175 one is able to relish the most sumptuous works of religious art from the 10th to the 15th centuries, with an astonishing mixture of classical Western and fabulous Oriental influences.

NOTRE DAME DE PARIS

Immortalized by Victor Hugo, this silent witness to the upheavals and the glory of French history symbolizes the heart of Paris. Both the Paris of kings and that of the ordinary people, milling about on the forecourt. From the medieval Mystery Plays to the crowning of Napoleon, from Quasimodo and Esmeralda to the *Te Deum* chanted at the Liberation, Notre Dame has throbbed, wept and sung with the rest of France.

On the site where it stands, on the Ile de la Cité—anchored in the middle of the Seine and representing the historic core of the capital—there were already two churches in the 10th century.

Work began in 1163. The definitive form of the choir was completed in 1177, and the extended nave in 1180. The first services were held in the new church in 1182 and it became fully operational by 1185.

With its brilliant new stained glass windows and splendid flying buttresses, the cathedral of Notre Dame was ready to enter the history of France. It was restored only once, by Viollet-le-Duc and Lassus, between 1845 and 1864; they restored some low-reliefs and the great spire, which had been damaged during the Revolution, when the cathedral was used as a short-lived "Temple of the Supreme Being" and of the "Cult of Reason".

After Senlis (1156) and Soissons (1160), Notre Dame is the oldest French religious building designed in keeping with the rules of the new Gothic style, which was beginning to supplant the traditional Romanesque. Actually the term "ogival" would be more suitable than "Gothic", which was reserved for Italian architecture between the Romanesque period and the Renaissance. Notre Dame is the best and the most perfect expression of this style in France.

The layout is in the shape of a cross: 422 feet long and 130 wide across the façade and 156 along the transept. The heights of the vaulted ceiling, the towers and the central spire are respectively 107, 225 and 293 ft. The enormous nave, its solid columns with floral capitals bearing a row of galleries, is illuminated by tall windows

which still have some of the original brilliant 12th-century stained glass windows.

The exterior is noted for its west façade. The triple porch is a masterpiece of harmony and elegance. In the center is the main portal of the Judgment (1220-31) restored by Viollet-le-Duc, who rebuilt part of the tympanum. The north portal, named after the Virgin, is the oldest of all (1210-20) and still has some of the original low-reliefs. On St. Anne's portal to the south, there are a number of authentic 12th-century sculptures. There is also a side door at each end of the transept which is almost as large and ornate as those on the façade.

Overhead is the Gallery of the Kings, which consists of a frieze-like arcade of 28 statues of the king of Judah and Israel.

The centrally located giant rosette window

(31 ft. in diameter), one of the finest windows in European Gothic art, is framed by two delicate blind arcades with fine columns. The base of the towers is linked by the great gallery, a high and delicate fringe of extremely elegant fine arcades, with the famous gargoyles protruding from its balustrade.

The tall and narrow bays add a graceful, light touch to the plain square towers. Both of them end in a terrace with a balustrade. The south tower houses the great bell, weighing 13 tons, which was built in 1440 and recast under Louis XIV.

The spires and arches, of the Cathedral of Notre Dame in Paris.

THE ARC DE TRIOMPHE

The upheavals and excesses of the interminable French revolution had left Paris in a deplorable state. As a result of the strain placed on the public finances by Napoleon's military ambitions and imperial megalomania, Paris looked more or less the same in 1815 as it had in 1715. The streets were still dirty, narrow and dark: the houses were huddled together, without sewers, light or hygiene.

Despite the spectacular recovery of trade and industry, spurred on by the ceaseless wars which made the city richer and more heavily populated, the emperor was so preoccupied with prestige and majesty that urban planning, for him, meant nothing more than the construction of grandiose buildings designed to glorify the emperor and his army, which was crucial to his power.

From 1806 onwards the architects of the period were to interpret Napoleon's thinking faithfully and brilliantly.

This sober, elegant yet solid architecture borrowed from the ancient world was intended as a symbol of power, authority and grandeur.

The grandest and most famous of these symbols was the Arc de Triomphe at the Etoile. The emperor commissioned Chalgrin to build it, and work began on August 15, 1806.

The Etoile de Chaillot had been so named since 1730, and had been laid out by Colbert on the former Colline du Roule, which had been leveled. In those days there were only five radiating avenues, the building of the others being decided as part of the gigantic plans of Baron Haussmann, in 1854, under the Second Empire.

They are what gives the Arc de Triomphe its exceptional setting with its splendid divergent avenues and unique view along the Champs-Elysées and the Concorde.

The arch was planned and begun by Chalgrin, whose work was continued by Blouet

and Huyot. By 1814, however, because of the great difficulties encountered by the empire only a rudimentary 20-ft section of the arch had been built.

Work resumed only in 1825, and was not completed until 1836, under Louis Philippe, while the decorative sculptures had to wait until 1844 before they were placed in position.

Grandeur, not originality, is the main feature of the Arc de Triomphe. This massive structure is copied from the arches of ancient Rome, and consists merely of two huge pillars supporting the gigantic arch. It is 156 feet tall, 146 wide and 98 from ground to vault. Its perfect proportions, enhanced by small lateral arches which relieve the pillars, manage to make this massive hulk as harmonious as it is powerful. Its main merit is that it embodies the most remarkable set of sculptures from the early 19th century.

Paris. The Arc de Triomphe. Left: the Place de l'Etoile and the Arch as visible from the Champs-Élysées. Below: the Tomb of the Unkown Soldier.

EIFFEL TOWER

In order to celebrate the centenary of the Revolution with all due magnificence, President Jules Grévy decided to organise a particularly memorable international World Fair in Paris in 1889. A monument, intended to represent France as brilliantly as possible, was to be chosen in an international competition.

Seven hundred candidates submitted designs. The winner was Gustave Eiffel, who proposed to build an extraordinary metal tower 984 feet tall, the like of which had never previously been seen.

Gustave Boenickhausen, alias Eiffel, was

Paris. The Eiffel Tower looming above the Seine and the Military Academy. Opposite: the view from the first of the tower's platforms.

trained as an engineer. By the age of 35, this dynamic and ambitious man had founded his own engineering company at Levallois. It was not long before his exceptional organising ability attracted attention. His speciality was the assembly of metal bridges, designed like immense Erector sets and completed at record speed on account of the high quality of the preliminary studies and a perfect mastery of advanced prefabrication.

As soon as the decision had been taken to build his design (January 1887), the Tower promptly began to arouse storms of protest, sarcastic comment and hostility, even before it was actually built.

Construction began, nonetheless, in 1887, under the watchful eye of Eiffel, helped by

Nougier, Koechlin and the architect Sauvestre. Progress was difficult, particularly in work on the 46-ft concrete foundations, because of water seepage from the nearby Seine.

In two years, however, the structure, which stands astride the Champ de Mars, between the Military Academy and the river, was completed—in the middle of the exposition of which it was the centerpiece. The centennial of the Revolution was inaugurated on 13 March 1889 by Sadi Carnot, the new President of the Republic, and Floquet, his Prime Minister.

From the start, the Eiffel Tower was a tremendous success. It consists of a pyramid resting on four solid pillars, built like the piers of a bridge, and converging towards a first platform.

Beyond that, the pillars grow thinner and taper towards the second platform, before eventually meeting to form a single pillar supporting the narrow landing at the top.

The Eiffel Tower was a bold venture which came to symbolize the triumph of metallic architecture in the 20th century.

The Centre Pompidou attracts more visitors than any other public building in Paris.

Paris. Place Beaubourg and the Centre Pompidou.

BEAUBOURG

As an illustration of the architectural use of iron, which was later to be more fully developed by Eiffel, the Paris Halles deserved to be left intact for posterity. Yet the decision to demolish them was taken in 1962, confirmed in 1968, and put into effect in the summer of 1971.

Georges Pompidou had chosen to turn the area into a cultural forum in the ancient manner, the throbbing heart of which would be a center for art and contemporary culture in the very middle of historic Paris. The competition to find a suitable design for this center was won by the architects Piano and Rogers. Preparation started in March 1973 and work on the infrastructure got under way in December 1972. The assembly of the metal structure took seven months (December 1974–June 1975) and on 8 January 1977 the Palais Beaubourg was opened to the public.

The building itself occupies only half of the esplanade cleared during preparatory demolition work, the rest being left deliberately empty in order to serve as a forum and a meeting place.

The Center was built on a strictly rectangular plan along rue du Renard. One part is under ground, while the rest consists of five levels of a strange tubularmetallic structure which forms merely a skeleton.

The floors are simply flat open areas 558 ft long, 48 wide and 23 high. Bundles of cables are attached to the floor, which is 5 1/2 inches thick. There are no fixed partitions. Moreover, each level is entirely transparent, with glass panels acting as walls between the metal braces.

Under ground the Center has an Institute for research in musical acoustics, while the other floors include libraries, bookshops, lecture and exhibition halls and an original Center for Industrial Creation.

At the last minute it was decided to set up in the Center the Museum of French Modern Arts, the showpiece of this temple of contemporary culture.

The esplanade outside the building is certainly serving as a forum: buskers, jugglers, musicians, painters and artists have moved into it in force. Art and creativity are thus mingled with the city itself, and brought directly to the people, just as in the Middle Ages when the mystery plays were performed on the forecourts of the cathedrals.

This monumental Erector set building marks a new phase in contemporary architecture: metal tubes have replaced beams, and glass is to be found everywhere, to impart transparency.

VERSAILLES

Early in the 17th century, when Louis XIII, a keen hunter, slipped away from the Louvre to track deer and boars at Versailles, the area consisted merely of a tiny hamlet surrounded by marshy moors and virgin forest. The king grew so fond of it that in 1630, when he was only 22, he decided to build a modest hunting lodge.

Nine years later, in 1631, he commissioned Philibert le Roy to build a second, larger structure of stone interspersed with brick and tiled with slate. When he was young, Louis XIV spent many happy hours on this royal estate. In 1661 he decided to transform it into a sumptuous castle, on a vast scale —the kind of thing that had never been seen before— to proclaim the absolute power of his monarchy.

Construction, which cost the enormous sum of 65 million *livres,* lasted throughout his reign; indeed it is quite true that Louis XIV, while at Versailles, lived perpetually in a construction site. The brilliant architect Le Vau was commissioned to design the palace; by the time of his death in 1670, he had completed its central part, to which he imparted an original style, French classicism, which thereafter became the European model. The 195-ft long central pavilion, with its enormous terrace, faced the new gardens, while serving as a setting, on the town side, for a delicate marble court.

Hardouin-Mansart was entrusted with the continuation of Le Vau's work. He added two

large wings, recessed in relation to the central pavilion, which he raised by one story, with a receding roof, thus creating his famous Mansard roofs. At the same time he covered the terrace to make the famous Galerie des Glaces. The definitive façade, opening into the garden, then measured 626 yards.

From 1661 to 1668, Le Notre and a group of the best hydraulic experts of the day (Girardon, Coysevox and the Massy brothers) laid out the park and a number of fabulous classical gardens; these are symmetrically arranged in relation to Le Vau's perron and the astonishing central view along the stretches of water, the lawns, the pond of Apollo and the Grand Canal (one mile long).

Marble and bronze statues from a mythological world of gods and heroes, made by Le Brun in association with the best sculptors of the day, were situated everywhere, between the shrubs and the ponds and along the geometrically laid out paths. Modern visitors are quite as enchanted by the stately perspectives of lawns, gardens and

water as was the court in the 18th century.

The interior of the château is richly adorned with a brilliant array of marble, wainscoting, molding, gilded furniture, *objets d'art* and precious ceramics.

The Trianons were built later, deep inside the park. The Grand Trianon (1687), by Mansart, was intended as a place where Louis XIV could go to escape the rigors of courtly life. Napoleon often stayed there. Now, furnished in the Empire style, it is still used as a residence for visiting heads of state.

The Petit Trianon, a plain pavilion built in 1755 by Mme Pompadour, was enlarged by Louis XV for Mme Dubarry. It became the favorite abode of Marie-Antoinette, who built the Hameau (hamlet) in the park (1775-84); it was here that she loved to play the shepherdess, in a setting reminiscent of the pastoral scenes from the paintings of Boucher and Fragonard.

During the Revolution the palace was sacked and looted. Years of patient and meticulous research and dedicated effort were needed before its original beauty could be restored.

The Palace of Versailles and statue of King Louis XIV at the entrance to the Court of Honour. Left: some of the gardens and the Grand Trianon.

MONT SAINT-MICHEL

Mont Saint-Michel, anchored inside its bay on the borders of Normandy and Brittany, is one of the most picturesque and interesting sites in the whole of France. It is a pyramid-shaped granite islet 260 feet tall and with a base 975 yards in circumference. Linked to the mainland by a long causeway, it is surrounded by water only at high tide. The rest of the time it towers over the shifting mud and sand banks which are gradually silting up the mouth of the bay and over the glistening and meandering riverlets which are a haven for water fowl.

In the eighth century, under Childebert, the rock—then known as Mont Tombe—was bare and deserted. By the year 707, however, there was already a hermitage at its summit. It was perhaps this that gave Bishop Aubert the idea of building an abbey in honor of Saint Michael on it; and the site itself must surely have reminded the prelate of the Monte Gargano shrine, where the Archangel was venerated in a rocky grotto. Indeed he brought certain relics from this latter sanctuary for the consecration of his abbey church.

During the Gothic period Mont Saint Michel suffered a severe setback: on 20 September 1421, under the administration of Cardinal d'Estouteville, the Romanesque choir collapsed. In 1448 it was replaced by a splendid flamboyant Gothic choir, and the monks took advantage of the new construction to rearrange their ancillary buildings.

The "Merveille" was transformed. On the first floor the almonry was still used to receive pilgrims, but on the floor above two remarkable rooms were built: the Salle des Hôtes (Guests' Room), which was set aside for visiting dignitaries, was designed as two vaulted naves with fine molded columns. These elegant touches add a considerable feeling of lightness to the Gothic style of the whole. Next to it is the Salle des Chevaliers, in a very different style, with much thicker, stout though highly ornate columns. Both have enormous fireplaces and ingenious latrines, cleverly taking advantage of the natural gradient of the rock.

On the upper floor, at the same level as the abbey church itself, is a cluster of communal facilities: the refectory, illuminated through tall slender windows, and the cloister, which has between its granite walls 127 fine and delicate columns made of a pink stone from England. Hidden under the Gothic structures is a rather touching little crypt consisting of a tiny pre-Romanesque double nave—all that remains of the original sanctuary.

In the 15th century the Mount was fortified and strengthened with thick towers and posterns, the better to resist the raids of the English, who held positions only two miles away on the small island known as Tombelaine. Yet the tiny village below the abbey, clinging to the rocky slopes, was never taken. Defended by a hundred Norman knights, the site proved to be impregnable.

Having been turned into a State prison during the Revolution, Mont Saint-Michel recovered its religious vocation in the 19th century.

The harshness of the bare rock is still relieved by a number of delightful and surprising terraced gardens.

From the Porte du Roi at the foot of the rock, up to the great staircase known as the Grand Degré, whose 90 steps lead up to the platform of the abbey, the medieval village (15th-16th centuries) climbs the steep slopes as far as the rampart walk, which provides visitors with a superb view of the bay 260 feet below and the picturesque rooftops.

Above the abbey a huge statue of the Archangel Michael, over 500 feet above the sea, spreads its protective wings skywards, for distant mariners to see, as if proclaiming to God the magnificent feats accomplished in his name by the faith and the genius of men.

Mont Saint-Michel. Below: a close-up of the design of the Basilica.

THE TOWER OF LONDON

More laden with history than the Bastille, and more steeped in legend than the Tour de Nesles, the famous Tower seems to cast a spell over all who visit it. Its sinister walls exude such an air of cloak-and-dagger intrigue and sinister plotting that for many people this will remain their most vivid memory of London.

Apparently Caesar had chosen this site, because of the strategic importance of its riverside location, for the first fortress which was erected there. But it was William the Conqueror who built the large square keep now in the center of the Tower, about 1078. The name White Tower is due to the limestone of which it was built and which was shipped specially from Caen. The Norman ruler sought to make it a solid defensive bastion and nothing more. But the outline of the keep is softened by the fine corner turrets, capped by elegant pinnacle turret roofs; the almost graceful effect thus achieved is enhanced by the tall and delicate weathercocks which make its silhouette even more slender.

His successors, especially William II (Rufus), added outer walls, towers, princely quarters and chapels, making it a forbidding citadel which could, nonetheless, serve as a residence.

Of the two concentric defensive walls, enclosing 12 ½ acres of paved courtyards, tortuous passageways and underground chambers, only the inner wall is strengthened with towers: it has thirteen of them, stout, round military bastions which could be used, depending on the needs of the day, as princely dwellings or top security cells.

The overall effect is one of an impressive and grim fortress-cum-palace, of considerable architectural value, as there are quite few well-preserved Norman citadels in existence. While the White Tower has been darkened by weathering over the centuries, the rest of the Tower of London is inherently gloomy and sinister. At a fairly early stage it ceased to serve as a residence, royal mint or law courts, and became specialized in a new role: that of State prison and barracks.

The most famous captive of the White Tower itself was Charles d'Orléans, captured at the Battle of Agincourt (1415), who spent 25 years within its walls, where he wrote the greater part of his melancholy poems.

Without a doubt the grimmest of all royal jails was the frightful Bloody Tower, which was added to the enclosure in the 14th century and was used for two centuries as a kind of executioner's waiting room. All the monarchs from Henry VIII to Elizabeth I kept those they were anxious to get rid of waiting there. Few of its inmates escaped the axe. In 1399 Richard II was imprisoned there after being ousted by Parliament. In 1483 Richard III had his two nephews, young Edward V and his brother the Duke of York, assassinated in the Bloody Tower. And Henry VIII had two of his rejected wives, Anne Boleyn (1536) and Catherine Howard (1542) incarcerated and then beheaded there. It was where Mary Tudor disposed of Jane Gray (1554), and where Elizabeth I imprisoned the famous navigator Sir Walter Raleigh, once her favorite (1592), and another favorite, Robert of Essex, who was less fortunate, being not only imprisoned but also beheaded (1601).

The mangled remains of the victims were brought back to tiny St. Peter's Chapel, near the place of execution, which was itself marked in the courtyard by a chilling brass plate. The names of those executed, however, were carved on the church door. In 1674 the bones of two children were found under the stairs in the tower: Charles II, thinking that they must have belonged to the nephews of Richard III, had them buried in

Westminster Abbey. The most recent prisoner was Rudolph Hess, who was imprisoned during the war in Beauchamp Tower.

The general mood is somewhat lightened, however, by the contents of Wakefield Tower: the Crown Jewels. This priceless treasure, dazzlingly arrayed in its glass prison, includes the most famous precious stones in the world: the rubies of the Black Prince, worn by Henry V at Agincourt; the Star of Africa, the biggest diamond known (530 carats), set in the royal scepter; and the Koh-i-Noor, worn only by queens.

Outside, the Yeomen of the Guard, in Tudor costume, continue their anachronistic rounds. They no longer even disturb the calmly familiar crows which have long resided with the Tower's walls; indeed the only event which has dislodged them, within living memory, was the air raids of 1941.

Several yards away the expressionless Thames flows quietly past these dread walls, which are so heavily charged with history.

The Tower of London on the banks of the Thames — its annexes, gardens, and fortifications. A singularly sturdy enclosing wall.

LONDON, THE PALACE OF WESTMINSTER

The astonishing thing about London is the fact that its historic buildings are widely scattered and that there is no Old Town, such as exists in the other great cities of Europe. This is doubtless due to the inability of the monarchy to influence official architecture and to the random growth of the city over the centuries, without an overall development plan.

At the end of the Roman occupation, however, the town was neatly enclosed within fortified walls, though it was of only minor political importance at the time.

The first royal Anglo-Saxon palace seems to have been the one built by King Canute, early in the 11th century, on the site of the present Parliament. It was destroyed, 30 years before the Norman conquest, by one of those devastating fires which periodically razed public buildings, and was rebuilt by Edward the Confessor (1042), who chose this rustic setting, outside the walls, for its peace and serenity.

William the Conqueror, whose reign was the true beginning of the rise of British power, moved into it after the Battle of Hastings (1066). But, finding this Anglo-Saxon palace rather crude by comparison with the princely French residences which he had known, he had it enlarged and embellished. In so doing he chose the severe and sober style of the Scandinavian houses of his ancestors.

It was William II (Rufus) who built the remarkable Westminster Hall (1097), which was altered by Richard II late in the 14th century. Thus completed, Westminster Palace remained the residence of the kings of England until Henry VIII (1509-1547). Shortly afterwards, the new occupants of Westminster were not the sovereigns, who had moved to Whitehall, but the elected assemblies, and the palace became a parliament.

The House of Commons was set up in the former St. Stephen's Chapel, whereas the Lords sat in the Chamber of Requests until a terrible fire

destroyed the building in 1834.

Visitors to London are amazed to find out that the present Houses of Parliament date only from the 19th century, whereas their stonework has weathered to such an extent as to suggest that they were built in the Middle Ages. Completed in 1888, they are the result of collaboration between two architects, Pugin and Barry, who built them in the purest flamboyant Gothic style, which was so fashionable during the Tudor period. The influence of the Town Halls of Louvain and, particularly, of Brussels is evident, as they also have tall façades with semi-embedded colonnades and ornate corner turrets. Fortunately the architects were able to incorporate what had been

saved and recovered from earlier buildings: a 13th-century crypt, a cloister built by Henry VIII in the 16th century, and, most particularly, the admirable nave of Westminster Hall, with its carved oak doors, which was built during the reign of the sons of William the Conqueror, in 1097.

In 1941 air raids gutted the House of Commons, which was carefully rebuilt in 1950 in accordance with the original plans.

The clock tower, which is 320 ft. tall, contains the famous Big Ben, a famous bell named after the man who built it, Sir Benjamin Hall, a man of legendary corpulence and joviality. Its 13 ½ tons of bronze have come to symbolize

London. The more distinguished House of Lords is crowned by Victoria Tower, a thick keep-like structure framed by four ornate turrets.

Nearby, Parliament Square, with its statues of famous men, adds a touch of gentleness and peace in this austere historic setting. The best view of Westminster Palace is had from Westminster Bridge. Seen across a misty Thames, this noble building, which despite its virtually new stone has a venerable past, lacks neither charm nor poetry.

London. Parliament and the Throne Room. The riverside skyline by night and London's historic center.

THE CANALS OF AMSTERDAM

Originally an ordinary village of fishermen and merchants, *Amstel-dam* ('dike on the Amstel') did not begin its commercial development until the 14th century. Very soon, however, on account of its religious tolerance—merchants from Antwerp and then Jews from Spain and Portugal took refuge there—and its control over the Dutch East Indies, it became one of the major metropolitan trading centers of Europe.

Its supremacy was also due in large part to the construction of a port on the Ij, by means of the extension of an artificial island 2 1/2 miles long, while to the east it connected with the land by the Ij.

What first strikes the visitor is the regular organization of the canals, which are laid out in a fan-like pattern around the geometrical center of the city, which is now occupied by Central Station. The aquatic spiderweb thus formed consists essentially of concentric and parallel canals. The Singel Gracht, on the periphery of the city encloses four concentric canals: the Kaiser Gracht (Canal of the Emperor), the Prinsent (Canal of the Princes), the Herrengracht (Canal of the Lords) and, in the center, the Singel.

Although their width varies from 65 to 45 ft, their average depth is only 8 ft. Along the elm-lined banks, the boats glide past rows of superb mansions built for the rich merchants of the 16th and 17th centuries. The finest of these have gables, redans and pediments; many have a pulley on an iron bar protruding from the top of the façade, to hoist loads which could not be moved up the steep and narrow Dutch stairs inside.

Built in the 16th and 17th centuries, of red brick, these houses have a generally somber hue which is enlivened by yellowish door and window frames and brightly colored shutters.

There are more than 400 bridges across the waterways of Amsterdam. The Old Town is considered to be everything inside the Singel Gracht, while the outlying districts which make

up the rest comprise modern Amsterdam.

Water, the source of the city's prosperity, is its dominant element. As one ambles along the canalways one can imagine oneself whisked aboard a trading vessel just in from the Indie sand about to unload its cargo of silks, teas, and spices at the city's very heart.

Such treasures were stored in ornate old buildings with pulley systems — the warehouses of those countless merchants who made up the slick entrepreneurial class and who, with their wide-brimmed hats and silver-buckled black shoes, featured so preminently on artists' canvases that were produced not so very far away in some of Europe's most famous studios.

Amsterdam's charm can best be savoured by wandering along those canals, for it is here that one recaptures that intimate, lively, lush and subtle magic that sheated this most paradoxical town — a town which, while stiffly conservative and bourgeois, was yet steeped in the lure of adventure and fortune's fancy that came wafted in on currents from beyond, beyond and from the Indian Ocean.

Two Amsterdam canals and the Montelbaan Tower.

BRUSSELS' CITY HALL

The heart of the old town, the "Grand'Place" — a regular oblong measuring 360 ft. by 223 — remains Brussels' prime tourist attraction to this day.

Built back in the 12th century on a stretch of drained marshland that flanked the original city limits, it soon became a thriving marketplace.

From the 13th century on, a compulsion for rectilinear construction dictated the square's present dimensions.

In the 17th century, with the completion of the Guilds and the king's mansion — formerly the bread pavilion, all built in the strictest Brabantine tradition of Italian classicism combined with Flemish flamboyance, the "Place" eventually acquired its bright, picturesque and lavish look, not to mention that remarkable architectural homogeneity that lends it such grace and charm.

One could hardly have imagined a more perfect site back in the early 15th century than this pure and exuberant Baroque setting for the new City Hall, or what was to re-establish the center of Brussels and, later, thrill even modern-day citizens with a legitimate sense of pride. It is a perfect example of the Brabant style in secular architecture. Its façade looks over the square which acts as its setting, and of which it is the outstanding component.

On first seeing this remarkable building, one is instantly captivated. This symphony of stone and lavish ornament has monumental dimensions and perfect proportions which give it a majestic grandeur; yet, despite the opulence with which it is decorated, the total effect is surprisingly sober.

Its belfry, the finest in Belgium, is a masterpiece of elegance and refined purity.

The left part of the Town Hall was built by Jacques Van Thieven, starting in 1402, when Brussels was at the height of its prosperity. The right wing was built later, probably in 1444, by Charles the Bold, who was then Comte du Charolais. The 312 ft-belfry-tower is the work of Jean Van Ruysbroeak (1449). At its top there is a 16-ft-gilded copper statue of Saint Michael slaying the dragon, somewhat in the position of a weathercock, which is the work of Martin Van Rode (1454).

Each of the four corners of the perfect rectangle formed by this building is nicely enhanced by a graceful and delicately ornate turret. The high and steeply sloping roof is bordered by ornamental battlements and by four rows of skylights, which lighten its general appearance.

This superb building, which was chosen by Charles V for his abdication in 1555, was seriously damaged by the artillery of the troops of Louis XIV. The ornamentation of the façade was enriched by a number of statues and sculptures which were added during the 19th century, and also by copies of original low-reliefs now in the Musée de la Braderie, representing the quintessence of the Brussels School in the 14th and 15th centuries, the period of its creative heyday. Classical themes had yielded to scenes of everyday inspiration, harshly perceptive as in the case of the 'men stacking chairs' or 'the drunken monks', which are the subject of some curious non-religious capitals.

Brussels. Building façades along the Grand' Place, and the City Hall.

COLOGNE CATHEDRAL

Cologne (German Köln) carries the key to its origins within its name, which derives from the Latin *colonia*. In 50 BC the Rhine marked the limits of Roman influence, and the Roman province of Gaul. Beyond lay territory which, if not actually unknown, was certain to involve adventure for those bold enough to enter it; it is for that reason that the Romans established nothing more substantial than *coloniae* there.

For the same reason, it was, during the Middle Ages, a prominent imperial city, a member of the Hanseatic League which grew immensely wealthy through the Baltic trade. An aristocracy of merchants and craftsmen, particularly goldsmiths, became very powerful and contributed greatly to the city's prosperity. Cologne in those days was certainly a political and economic force to be reckoned with, and its Archbishop was a Grand Elector of the Empire.

Saint Peter's Cathedral, known locally as the Dom, had succeeded, in the 13th century, an initial 9th-century Carolingian church built on a man-made mound formed from the rubble of earlier Roman buildings.

Its dimensions are majestic, but very well proportioned. The facade, which is nearly 200 feet wide, is dominated by two imposing four-story towers, 520 feet tall; the first two stories are based on a square plan, and the upper two are octagonal. From the outside, one's attention is most taken by the south porch and the choir. Whereas the choir which, set among a forest of slender flying buttresses relieves the enormous thrust of the vaults, dates from the 14th century, the decorative sculpture on the porch is modern, as are the bronze and mosaic doors, which were made during restoration work between 1948 and 1953.

The interior is striking because of the incredible vertical thrust of its remarkably graceful pillars. The choir still has the earliest original decoration of the 14th-century structure: statues of the apostles, the finely wrought canonical stalls, and the high altar (1320), of black marble enhanced with white statuettes.

But the finest piece of all is the reliquary of the Three Magi said to contain their relics; this finely carved masterpiece of the goldsmith's art, in the form of a basilica with three naves, was made by François Nicolas de Verdun late in the 12th century. The rest of the cathedral is a genuine museum: some ten chapels contain priceless gems of religious art: sarcophagi, reclining figures, altar pieces, statues and triptychs. The extremely interesting stained glass windows date from between 1270 and 1320.

In the last months of the war the air raids, which miraculously spared the cathedral, uncovered the extraordinary Dionysos Mosaic, from Roman times, which covers more than 640 square feet and contains 31 pictures on which more than two million colored cubes were used.

This majestic and superbly decorated church is one of the finest examples of Gothic art.

BERLIN, THE BRANDENBURG GATE

The Brandenburger Tor, the most famous monument in Berlin, was built in 1788-89, under Frederick-William II, by the architect and sculptor C.G. Langhans.

The designers of this majestic triumphal arch which was based on the models of antiquity, including the Athenian propylea, were certainly determined to impress. Six pairs of sober fluted Doric columns are grouped around five porches: the one in the center is large, and the two located to either side are narrower. Above the pediment, which is decorated with a frieze of sculpted metopes, an auriga of gilded bronze drives a quadriga similar to those used by Roman generals when celebrating their triumphs. Four powerful horses, harnessed abreast, are drawing along to glory a winged hero clad in a peplum, a laurel crown on his brow, and proudly carrying a banner like those of the Roman legions. This group, the work of Shadow, completes the symbolic value of the triumphal arch of victorious Germany.

In the two centuries since it was erected, the Brandenburg Gate has seen the men who have influenced the destiny of their country, for better or for worse, file past on historic occasions.

Left: the exterior of the apse, at the Cathedral of Cologne. Above: the Triumphal Arch of the Brandenburg Gate in Berlin.

NURENBERG AND MUNICH

Ever since the spectacular Nazi Rallies (1933-39) of the Hitler era, and the War Crimes Tribunal (1945-46), the name of Nurenberg has been widely known throughout the world. The town was chosen in both instances for its symbolic significance, on account of its considerable importance in German history. In the Middle Ages the burgraves, who were in command of the imperial fortress and the founders of the principality, brought prosperity to Nurenberg, which enjoyed a superb geographical position, on the banks of the Peghitz and at the intersection of the major trade routes. It was even more influential during the 18th century—the high point of its history—because of the renown of its intellectuals, artists and scholars, who were among the most famous in all of Germany.

Among them were Hans Behaim, the town architect; the stone carver Adam Kraft (1450-1509); Albert Dürer, the most famous German painter (1471-1518); Veit Stoss, the eminent wood sculptor (1440-1533); and Peter Visher, the renowned bronze smelter (1455-1529). Not to forget Hans Sachs, the poet (1494-1576), nor the legendary Master Singers and the mythical Tannhauser, the 13th-century poet and warrior, who also inspired Wagner.

In the 15th century this creative ferment, so reminiscent of the Florence of the Medicis, gave rise to the prestige and wealth of the medieval town. A stout fortified wall encompassed in a single defensive system the two parts of the town which were separated and grouped about their respective churches, and which had formerly been enclosed within their own ramparts.

The heavy damage done by air raids during the war was carefully repaired in compliance with the original plans. It is worth noting, in this connection, that the medieval town planners who were responsible for the layout of the old town took exceptional pains to avoid the building of narrow winding streets and to allow only the finest of secular and sacred architecture.

The old town on the right bank is clustered around the 13th—century church of Saint Sebald.

North of this historic part of town, the hill with the castle looks down over a square bordered by some restored but very homogeneous 15th—and 16th—century houses, including the spectacular half-timbered house (1450-60) in which Albert Dürer lived from 1509 to his death in 1528.

The massive and imposing old imperial fortress (Kaiserburg), founded in the 11th century and enlarged by Frederick Barbarossa in the 12th, is the oldest and most venerable building in the town.

One might mention the imitation Flemish Gothic tower of the Munich Town Hall — from the start of the century — for the joyous peal of its bells that can be heard everyday at eleven o'clock, much as in days of old — or the animated, almost life-size figures of the Duke of Bavaria taking the and of a Lorraine princess in marriage.

Munich. City Hall, not far from the Cathedral. Opposite: figures in the carillon, within the central tower of this edifice. Left: the architectural splendors of the medieval City of Nüremberg.

THE CASTLES OF LUDWIG II

There is endless fascination in the personality of this king of Bavaria, a fervent admirer of Wagner and Louis XIV who pursued his musical fantaisies in a dream of stone which was often bizarre but which still astounds visitors to his fabulous castles.

The castle of Neuschwanstein was the first to be started by the sovereign, in 1869. The king was so delighted with its mountain setting, which is truly an exceptionally beautiful Alpine landscape, that he wrote to his god, Richard Wagner: "The place is inaccessible and sacred".

Perched at nearly 3,000 ft above sea level, on a rocky spur, it towers over the Pollat Gorges from the top of a sheer rock face. With its towers, turrets, pinnacle-turrets, watch-towers, machicolations and pepper-pots it is just like a castle from a fairy-story.

Its light-colored stones rise majestically from the dark firs, and form a colossal, unreal outline against the sky, as if Albert Dürer himself had drawn it there. This perfect symbol of the Germany of Goethe and Wagner is passionate and dramatic, superhuman and spellbinding.

In 1869 the architects, Dollmann and Riedel, set about this gigantic commission which was not to be completed by the time of the king's death in 1886.

After passing through the postern, visitors enter the courtyard where the palace, the heart of the castle, is situated. It is a powerful four-story building, framed by towers, which manages to be both imposing and graceful. The royal apartments, which are abundantly adorned with colonnades, wainscoting, moldings, joists and paintings, occupy the third floor. The *leitmotiv* running throughout the decor is the illustration of the works of Wagner: *Siegfried* in the lobby, *Tannhauser* in the royal study, *Lohengrin* in the state reception rooms, *The Master Singers* in the toilet and *Tristan and Isolde* in the bedroom.

He actually lived at Linderhof, at an altitude of nearly 3,000 ft. There, in another exceptional setting, he built a Rococo imitation of Le Trianon. Construction started after his visit to Versailles in 1874, and took five years to complete, as all the materials had to be brought in overland across very difficult terrain.

The interior, which was intended as a kind of "poetic asylum", extolls the glory of Ludwig's new gods: the dynasty of the Bourbons and France. The bust of Louis XIV reigns supreme in the vestibule, and, as in the royal bedroom at Versailles, he built a splendid baluster of gilded wood—an insurmountable symbolic rampart. This time, in order not to be disturbed during meals, he had the entire table hoisted up from the kitchen by powerful lift.

Ludwig used to withdraw frequently into his 75-acre park, where he had installed a Moorish kiosk which he had bought in Paris at the 1867 Exposition. He was also fond of the breathtaking Grotto of Venus, which had been carved specially from the rock: it has a shell-shaped throne, phosphorescent concrete drapes, a waterfall and an artificial lake.

Two of the extraordinary castles which King Louis II of Bavaria had constructed: Linderhof and Neuschwanstein.

PARLIAMENT BUILDING, BUDAPEST

Whether one arrives over land or along the Danube—certainly the most beautiful way to approach the city—one thing soon becomes evident: Budapest has no Old Town as such, not even on the slopes of the right bank where Arpad's Hungarians first settled. The only evidence of the history of the capital is provided by Mount Var, site of the diffuse and heavy Royal Palace, founded by King Bela IV towards 1235, and the church of King Matthias (15th century). The absence of traces of the past is even more complete in Pest, on the left bank: here everything is modern, with no building at all older than the 19th century.

Yet one's attention is immediately arrested by the imposing outline of the Parliament Building. As soon as the city acquired the rank of capital, a decision was taken to build it as a pledge of independence and national sovereignty.

It is a gigantic building covering a total of more than 870 ft. along the Danube waterfront and opening onto the 16 acres of the equally huge Kossuth Square, which it shares with the old Law Courts, now an ethnographic museum, and the Ministry of Agriculture.

The new building, which was completed in 1886, was required above all to be majestic and impressive. This fact accounts for the choice of a very florid neo-Gothic style and the unmistakable influence of the Houses of Parliament in London, as well as the Town Halls of Brussels and Louvain.

Bristling with spires and pinnacle turrets, and covered with tall pointed roofs, it was clearly

intended primarily as a symbol for the Hungarian nation, with the emphasis on ornamental effects and magnificence.

Its architect, Steindl, did not hesitate to draw on the well proven motifs of Venetian and Byzantine ornamentation in order to make it even more impressive and attractive. The result is an enormous, complex and rather heterogeneous building whose main merit is ornate grandeur and

flamboyant majesty.

The wings, each covered by a roof flanked by four spires, used to house the parliamentary assemblies: the Upper Chamber to the north and the National Assembly to the south. The former throne room, in the center, crowned by a huge cupola 320 ft tall, with strong Byzantine overtones, has now become the President's Council Room.

Above: the Parliament in Budapest, and Charles Bridge in Prague (with the Hradcany Palace in the background). Opposite: the Cathedral of Saint Stephen in Vienna.

PRAGUE, THE CHARLES BRIDGE

The Town with a Hundred Towers, where each stone has its history: this is how its inhabitants think of the old town within their capital city.

Built on a rocky spur on the left bank of the Moldau (Vlatva) River, Mala Strana was the aristocratic part of Prague. At the foot of the castle, with some fine secular and religious buildings of the 13th century, was the residential quarter of the notables and leading burghers, who filled it with opulent palaces and sumptuous patrician mansions, nestling deep inside stately parks.

The right bank was the Gothic and Baroque town of merchants and artisans: Stare Mesto, the old 15th-century hamlet, with its winding streets, arcaded squares and massive vaults. The new quarters, Nove Mesto, fortunately grew southwards, towards the plain, sparing the picturesque old town. By the 11th century Prague was a rich commercial town, very much involved in the business life of Central Europe. In the 13th century it was the capital of Bohemia and in the 15th, that of the Germanic Holy Roman Empire. In those days, when it was at the peak of its greatness, it was the most beautiful city in Central Europe. Charles Bridge, which links the old town of Stare Mesto across the Moldau to the historic quarter of Mala Strana, was and still is its finest structure.

Charles Bridge, the pride of Prague, was started by Peter Parler in 1357; it is 1680 feet long and has 15 piers. At the time it was part of the great medieval highway which crossed the country, and was therefore of considerable strategic importance. Its construction was a superb technical feat, and from an esthetic point of view it is also exceptional, showing a high degree of craftsmanship and artistic taste. Its fame is due to the double row of statues which still adorn its parapets. The oldest of these, dating from the 15th century, depicted Roland and the martyrs' pillar. In 1683 St. John Nepomucenus was added, and, from 1796 to 1714, 26 other sculpted groups were also placed in position.

The most famous of them include Saint Luitgard (by the Czech sculptor Matthias Braum) and particularly the Turk, by Brokoff, sculpted in 1714 in honor of the Trinitarians who redeemed Christian prisoners being held by the Turks.

By 1714 only two spots were left vacant: they were occupied by Saint Christopher (1857) and Wenceslaus (1859).

In this way the inhabitants since the 15th century have seen an extraordinary succession of statues taking their places on the parapets of this venerable bridge—statues of saints and kings, sprouting as strong as trees, sprightly and full of vigor.

Because of them, Charles Bridge is still the most exquisite place for a stroll in the whole of Prague. As one walks by one can appreciate the Baroque masterpieces, and at the same time enjoy the view of the Moldau and the picturesque little island of Kampa, with its old mills at the river's edge and its pottery market. At each end of the bridge there is a superb Gothic tower, bearing the seal of the stone-carvers.

VIENNA CATHEDRAL

The Cathedral stands on the small St. Stephen's Square, whose modest dimensions, inherited from the Middle Ages, nicely emphasize the vertical thrust of the spire. Moreover the maximum height of rooftops in the whole of the old town has remained at 82 ft. It is a Gothic building, with some interesting features:

The stone used to build its walls includes a number of tombstones from the old cemetery which surrounded it, as well as some Turkish cannonballs, a memento of the 1683 siege. A fine western façade, a remnant of the 13th century Romanesque cathedral, consists of an imposing portal surrounded by the two remarkable Towers of the Pagans (210 ft).

The superb central portal, the Riesentor, or Giant's Doorway, derives its name from the tibia bone of a mammoth which was found during excavations for the foundations—and which was later transformed by legend into the leg of a giant drowned by the Flood! On either side of this portal are two curious iron bars, set into the wall, which represent the standard measurements of the period: an ell and a double foot. According to tradition the hole in the stonework at the same place marked the standard size for the loaf of bread.

The gem of this cathedral is its belltower. This slender, delicate masterpiece, the tallest Gothic tower in the world, is intersected by some remarkable stone patterns. It took 74 years to build (1359-1433) and stands 445 ft above the square. A plain staircase leads up to a platform from which defenders used to watch for the Turks during the sieges and launch rockets to alert the Austrian armies to the imminent danger.

The Turks are no longer in evidence today, but there is a good view of the layout of the old town enclosed by the Ring, the boulevard which runs along the site of the old walls. This inner

area is the setting in which the Hapsburg saga took place. Its two poles remain the Hofburg and the old St. Stephen's Cathedral, surrounded by a tangle of delightful narrow streets which still have a distinct aura of centuries gone by.

Inside the Cathedral, as one might expect, there is the usual abundance of paintings, heraldic shields, rare marbles and stained glass windows.

Original features are the fine 16th century sculpted chair and the interesting catacombs which contain a number of sarcophagi of bishops and, in particular, the astonishing copper urns bearing the entrails of the Hapsburg family. As one gazes upon these macabre pot-bellied jars, in the damp penumbra of a Gothic crypt, one cannot fail to think back to the power that family once wielded in Europe, and to ponder on the Eternal Truths...

THE KREMLIN

The first palisade erected in 1156-58 by Yuri Dolgoruki to fortify the wooden escarpment which towers over the Moscow River from over 130 ft is now no more than a distant legend. The tiny fort, at the forest's edge, was the cradle of the future capital. In the 13th century it was consolidated and made into a proper fortress, with a tall and powerful girdle of crenellated ramparts reinforced by numerous towers (1484-1508).

The town thus became a bastion against the dangerous world of the steppe, as well as the symbol of the national power of young Russia. Having been ravaged, occasionally destroyed but always rebuilt, the Kremlin was soon a real fortified town, with its palaces, houses and churches. The present walls date from Dimitri Donskoi (1367). But each new reign and sovereign made their own architectural contribution, with varying degrees of success. However complex and lacking in homogeneity it may be, the Kremlin as a whole is truly the heart of Moscow and of all Russia.

The Kremlin is the 'Upper City'. In ancient times it would have been known as an Acropolis. Since 1495 its external outline has not changed, and its girdle of tall, fawn crenellated walls encloses an immutable triangle, one side of which is reflected in the protective waters of the river while the other faces Red Square, the starkness of which is relieved by the cupolas of Saint Basil's. This monumental cluster of buildings is heavy with symbolism: the symbolism of war, religion and State. These walls have harbored the conspiracies and massacres which formed the web of Russian history until the advent of Peter the Great (1689). Appalled by the plots and political murders which went on in the Kremlin, the new tsar abandoned Moscow, which he disliked intensely, and moved his capital to Saint Petersburg. It was not until 1918 that the Kremlin once again became the seat of government.

The red brick surrounding wall, which is over 7,000 ft long and between 16 and 65 ft high, depending on the terrain, is between 10 and 16 ft thick. It encompasses an area of 11 acres, containing palaces and churches. This formidable defensive structure is fortified by 20 strongly built towers. The most famous of these are the Spaskaya (Tower of the Savior; 230 ft; 1491), which was the entrance used by the tsar and his nobles; the Tower of the Senate (1491) and the Nikolskaya (Tower of Saint Nicholas) which looks down over Red Square. The Kutafia and Borovitskaya Towers are the present entrances to the Kremlin, in the Alexander Garden. One should not forget the elegant Vodozvodnaya Tower, which looks down over the river from which water used to be pumped to it for use in the gardens.

The interior is complex and heterogeneous. The Great Palace, built in 1753 for Nicholas I, is next to the Palace of the Facets, with its remarkable frescoes, and the Palace of the Armories, which contains the throne of Ivan the Terrible as well as a superb collection of weapons. In the old Senate, which was built under Catherine II, Lenin lived for more than five years, until his death.

The only homogeneity here is to be found in the charming and majestic cathedral square, which is surrounded by the principal churches of the Kremlin: the Collegiate Church of the Annunciation (1484-89), the private chapel where the tsars were baptised and married; the Cathedral of the Assumption (1475-79), more sumptuous than the others, in which the tsars were crowned (it contains the stall of Ivan the Terrible and sarcophagi of tsars and church patriarchs); the Collegiate Church of the Archangel (1505-09); the small church of the Deposition of the Robe of Our Lady; and the belltower of Ivan III the Great, which took a century to complete (1505-1600).

Wherever one looks there are admirable frescoes and wonderful icons. It is interesting to note that the palaces and churches of the Russia of the tsars were all designed by Italian architects and artists. This may account for the sensuous charm radiated by churches which, despite their rigid and even austere appearance on the outside, have interiors which convey a sumptuous fairytale quality.

Indeed, as the poet said: "Above Moscow there is the Kremlin; but above the Kremlin there is only heaven".

Moscow. Upper left: the Kremlin's array of cupolas. Opposite: the entrance to the collection of monuments that comprise the Kremlin. Right: Saint Basil's Cathedral on Red Square.

LENINGRAD, THE WINTER PALACE

Three centuries ago the place where the Winter Palace now stands was nothing but fields of rye, along the banks of the Neva. It was Peter the Great's dislike for Moscow and its Kremlin that led him to build the new capital of imperial Russia at this point.

Having been crowned in 1689, he started in May 1703 on the construction of the Peter and Paul Citadel, the defensive key to the future city. The Summer Palace was built in 1711; it is a comfortable but modest residence in which the sovereign sought to recreate the Dutch burgher milieu so dear to his heart. There was a most significant gap between the small scale of the house which the tsar wanted for himself and his grandiose projects for the future capital of Greater Russia.

A population was found for the new city by virtue of edicts and binding decisions taken from on high: merchants were obliged to build houses of stone; all barges had to carry a load of

been plotted behind these walls. Before the Revolution and the shooting of 9 January 1905 there had been a political fire which had proved quite as devastating as the disaster which had destroyed part of the building in 1837; restoration was done by Stasov, who preserved the Italian spirit sought by its builder-architect.

Together with four smaller buildings from the same period situated nearby, the Winter Palace has been dedicated to the cause of Art, since it comprises the Ermitage Museum, one of the finest in the world. In 1764 Catherine II had Vallin de Lamothe and Yuri Veltem build a smaller and more discreet Petit Ermitage next to the Winter Palace, for more intimate receptions. At same time, her passion for Western culture led her to buy 225 paintings in Berlin, thus forming the nucleus of the collections which she enriched every year with new and superb acquisitions in France and England. These paintings, the personal property of the sovereign, gradually invaded the rooms of the great palace.

It now contains 2,600 works from all over

building materials on each trip they made; whole populations were 'displaced' etc.

Saint Petersburg was to remain the heart of Russia until the Revolution. Elizabeth I and Catherine II, in particular, did much to enhance and perpetuate the city, which was permanently opened onto Europe. In 1905 the shooting on the Palace square and the storming of the Winter Palace itself, on 12 March 1918, finally put an end to the city's imperial history.

The superb and majestic Palace square, with Alexander's Column at its center, provides a grandiose setting which is well worthy of the colossal Winter Palace which closes it off like a massive backdrop, next to the classic Military Staff Building and the Admiralty with its distinctive spire.

The Winter Palace is an impressive building, constructed between 1754 and 1762 by Bartolomeo Rastrelli. It is a triumph of the sumptuous Italian Baroque style; its immense façade is enhanced by a majestic forest of marble columns with neo-classical capitals.

The whole place is on an extravagant, gigantic scale: 1,050 rooms, 1947 windows, 117 stairways, 1 1/2 miles of cornices and vast numbers of gilded statues.

For two centuries, Russian history has

the world, on display in 40 rooms. In this way the palace of Catherine the Great—the symbol of absolute power, and for a brief while between 1905 and 1917 the palace of the revolution—has become a maze of the world's painting. From salon to ante-chamber, between precious furniture and ceilings adorned with gilded stucco, in the midst of the majestic opulence of what was once one of the grandest royal residences in the world, one wanders through an incredible array of fabulous collections, ranging from the marvelous gold objects of the Scythians to the finest gems of Western painting. Spanish and Flemish, German and Dutch, French and English, they are all there, from Velasquez to Picasso, El Greco to Breughel, da Vinci to Renoir. The beauty of the setting is not alien to the pervasive charm of the palace's sumptuous rooms; one's eye, for example, may catch a glimpse, through the gilt molding of a window, of the green and impassive waters of the Neva, which has seen a great many changes as it has passed beneath these royal walls.

Leningrad. Above: Revolution Square, just in front of the Winter Palace. Right: another view of the palace.

EMPIRE STATE BUILDING

The cosmopolitan influx which began to reach New York in the 19th century, coupled with the city's exceptional prosperity, led to the adoption of original solutions in many spheres. The colonial architecture which had been imported from Europe was eventually superseded by a host of skyscrapers for which Manhattan is famous.

Pressure on the land made it more sensible to build upwards rather than outwards. The new architecture was aided providentially by Otis's invention of the elevator, and by new materials such as glass and steel which lightened the mass of concrete required.

The florid, baroque buildings from before the First World War, constructed with traditional techniques, deserved their nickname of 'Wedding Cakes'. But all that changed between the two wars: sheer and strictly vertical lines began to appear, while façades became flat, stark and geometrical. The resulting structure, however, was something of a fortress, almost a prison, lacking any symbiosis with the street on which it stood

and obscured by the gigantic scale of its own concrete and steel cliff faces. The Empire State Building, the oldest and still the most famous of the New York skyscrapers, dates from this first period of vertical architecture.

Its characteristic silhouette, ending in a huge conical antenna which seems to soar like an arrow from the heart of Manhattan, is visible for many miles around.

This remarkable building, which is 1,470 ft. tall, was completed in less than two years (1929-1931) by three architects—Shreve, Lambs and Harmon—and cost 40 million dollars. The amazing speed of construction was due to the revolutionary design and the materials used: long steel beams (60,000 tons in all!) were assembled like the pieces in an Erector set, on very solid foundations. Sometimes a whole floor was completed in a single day.

The Empire State has one hundred and two floors, ending in a stoutly built 223-ft. antenna, standing on a platform, which was once regarded as a potential berth for airships.

Keeping the 6,500 windows of this famous

building clean is a full-time job. A total of one hundred and fifty people are permanently engaged in cleaning, maintaining and providing security for this huge office building.

The 16,000 people who work in the Empire State Building, and its 3,500 daily visitors are conveyed by seventy-three elevators, some of which can reach the observation floor in less than a minute.

From the top there is a breathtaking view of New York harbor, the skyscrapers of midtown and downtown Manhattan, the four other boroughs of New York City and the outlying districts.

The fine decorative marble by Roy Sparkia and Renee Nemorov in the main lobby is the sole ornamental concession to be found in this admirable, yet chilling, temple of steel and glass.

New York. The Empire State Building. The needle atop the skyscraper.

WORLD TRADE CENTER

The center consists of six buildings of differing sizes, surrounding a large plaza (five acres). Every effort was made to humanize this new complex, by including areas of vegetation and fountains. The beautiful rotating bronze globe which stands in the middle of a pool in the plaza is the work of Fritz Koenig.

Above ground the plaza is wholly relaxing and peaceful, as all amenities and equipment have been kept in the first basement, where there is a shopping center and six floors of parking for a total of 2,000 cars.

The buildings themselves were erected around the sides of this immense well of air and light. Four low-rise buildings, with only 9 floors, contain the customs office, the sugar and coffee exchanges, banks and insurance companies. Only two of the Center's buildings are skyscrapers—twin 1,378-ft towers with 110 floors and foundations sunk 70 feet into the rock. Their sheer vertical ribbing, unbroken by ledges, gives them a kind of absolute purity of line—an effect which is deceptively simple but actually required a total

mastery of construction in metal and glass on this scale.

The frame consists of a gigantic stockade of steel columns only 22 inches apart; the windows are therefore immense slits. The façades are entirely covered with aluminium, which accounts for their characteristic and spectacular silvery sheen.

With its walls of glass or steel, aluminium or concrete, Manhattan has transformed the architectural thinking inherited from Europe and has succeeded in creating, out of sheer necessity, a highly contemporary urban setting, in which the shape of the future can already be discerned.

In less than 50 years New York moved from classicism to the Baroque, and on to the French Beaux-Arts before discovering the skyscrape which was to become its symbol.

New York. The International Trade Towers and a view of the mall below.

ROCKEFELLER CENTER

In the heart of Manhattan there is a harmonious group of tall buildings which truly constitute a 'city within the city'.

It is hard to imagine the site of Rockefeller Center as it was late in the 19th century. In those days it was a tranquil rustic landscape which so appealed to a Scottish professor from the University of Columbia that he bought it in 1880 with a view to building a botanical garden. The venture was too much for him, however, and he sold it back to the city of New York, which turned it into a quiet residential area much sought after by prominent citizens.

Although it was abandoned early in the 19th century because of the increase in mechanical noise as the city grew northwards, it experienced a second youth during the Prohibition years, as its abandoned houses were turned into clandestine bars.

At this point along came J.D. Rockefeller Jr, who took a lease on the whole area until the year 2060. He wanted to build a gigantic opera house, but the 1929 Wall Street crash forced him to change plans. He then turned to the idea of a business center, commissioning Wallace Harrison —later the designer of the UN Headquarters and Lincoln Center—to make it a reality.

Work proceeded rapidly and was virtually completed by 1940. It used to be said, uncharitably, that Rockefeller himself sometimes visited the site *incognito,* so as to check on the pace of construction by peering through a hole in the fence.

The Center consists of a central skyscraper surrounded by a dozen satellite buildings. The heart of the complex is the RCA building, which houses the broadcasting facilities of the NBC. It is 680 feet high and has 70 floors; its concrete sides, which taper as a result of broad ledges, are strongly reminiscent of the architecture of ancient Babylon. It is, in fact, rather like an elongated and stylized *ziggurat.*

This ultra-modern Tower of Babel dominates a group of buildings which are quite as appealing and graceful and which each have their own architectural personality and silhouette.

The Time-Life building (585 ft and 48 floors) has sheer walls of glass and aluminium. The MacGraw-Hill building (51 floors) is an elegant tower with shallow ledges. The Hilton (46 floors) and the Sheraton (50 floors) have large areas of glass over a concrete frame. The very refined International building (41 floors) has a lobby which is decorated in the style of antiquity with the most beautiful Greek marble from Tinos. The Exxon building (54 floors, 745 ft) is a starkly impressive tower whose sole ornamentation consists of the special angles built into one corner.

The urban texture of Rockefeller Center consists of a number of distinctly low buildings. All of the buildings are connected by a network of large underground galleries containing luxury stores, restaurants and entertainment facilities. There is even a skating rink next to the Channel Gardens, a veritable oasis with its ponds, statues and fountains. Carnegie Hall and the Museum of Modern Art are situated just outside the periphery of the area.

All in all, Rockefeller Center consists of 19 commercial buildings with 557 floors of offices and 60,000 employees. With the daily influx of visitors, that makes a total of 250,000 inhabitants of this city within a city.

New York. Rockefeller Center — the ice skating rink and the garden promenade through to Fifth Avenue, with a view of the main buildings.

GOLDEN GATE BRIDGE

In 1906 a terrible earthquake followed by a gigantic fire destroyed San Francisco. The disaster did, however, compel the architects to revamp their urban planning altogether, and the town was rebuilt in the neo-classical style in vogue at the time, and on the basis of a strict geometric plan.

The town is situated in a most majestic setting, on a large peninsula. Early in the century some thought was given to the possibility of linking the town to the hills which circle the bay. The Golden Gate Bridge was then built to span the Golden Gate, a strait separating the center of town from the marine peninsula. This must surely be the most famous bridge in the world; it is certainly the symbol of San Francisco, just as the Eiffel Tower symbolizes Paris.

Like the Tower, it is made of metal; it is over 1 1/2 miles long and 88 ft wide. It is suspended 228 ft above the sea; its pillars are 745 ft high and the thickness of the suspension cables is as much as 36 inches.

Though the decision to build it was taken in 1923, the bridge did not take shape until 1933; two years of studies were needed after the necessary capital had been raised. (1930).

The design was entrusted to Joseph Strauss, of Cincinnati, a visionary architect who had already designed more than 400 steel bridges in the USA as well as a fantastic project for a viaduct linking North America to northern Asia via the Bering Strait.

The strong currents in the Golden Gate made construction difficult. While the north pillar posed few problems, the south pillar, at the San Francisco end of the bridge, was a severe challenge. The divers could work only one hour at a time, four times a day, between tides. The force of the waves was so great that the workers were constantly being incapacitated by sea sickness, and the pontoon laden with equipment sometimes broke adrift and sank.

It eventually became necessary to build a tall concrete dike 33 ft thick and 66 ft high in order to isolate the working area and keep it dry. Strauss finally made a concrete base 40 ft tall, at the bottom of the coffer dam, in order to erect the south pillar. The installation of the cables was also difficult, because the fitters suffered greatly from vertigo.

This prodigious feat of engineering was inaugurated on 27 May 1937. Visitors to San Francisco, always impressed by the bridge's purity of line, are sometimes astonished by its color, a bright orange, permanently maintained by a squad of painters using two tons of minium each week.

Despite the considerable sway, which may be as much as 20 feet the middle of the bridge, its solidity has never failed. It was designed to resist stormy weather and has been closed only once, in 1953.

It is best to cross the bridge on foot to enjoy the splendid view it offers of the bay, while at the same time relishing the beauty of its pure lines. The sensation of floating in midair is enhanced by the mist which frequently hangs over the bay, adding a further touch of unreality to this enchanting bridge, hanging between heaven and earth.

Two glimpses of the Golden Gate Bridge in San Francisco. A segment of one of the bridge's suspension cables. Mermorial plaque recording completion of this towering structure.

DEDICATION
BY THE DIRECTORS
AND OFFICERS OF THE
GOLDEN GATE BRIDGE
AND HIGHWAY DISTRICT

IN THE YEAR 1937 NINETEEN YEARS AFTER ITS INCEPTION
THE GOLDEN GATE BRIDGE OF SAN FRANCISCO IS HERE
DEDICATED
TO THE PEOPLE OF THE GOLDEN GATE BRIDGE AND
HIGHWAY DISTRICT WHO GUARANTEED IT
TO THE CITIZENRY OF THE STATE OF CALIFORNIA
WHO SPONSORED IT
AND TO THE WORLD AT LARGE WHOSE ADVENTUROUS
SPIRIT IT REFLECTS

LIFTING ITS MIGHTY FORM HIGH ABOVE THE GOLDEN GATE
IT SHALL TESTIFY TO THE FAITH AND DEVOTION OF THOSE
WHO UNDAUNTED THROUGH THE YEARS
SOUGHT HONESTLY AND FAIRLY THROUGH THIS STRUCTURE
TO TENDER A DEFINITE CONTRIBUTION
TO THE CULTURAL HERITAGE OF MANKIND

CONCEIVED IN THE SPIRIT OF PROGRESS
IT SHALL STAND AT THE GATES OF SAN FRANCISCO
A MONUMENT TO HER VISION AN INSPIRATION TO
POSTERITY
AND AN ENDURING INSTRUMENT OF CIVILIZATION
FAITHFULLY SERVING THE NEEDS OF A QUICKENING WORLD

DEDICATION
BY
THE NATIVE SONS
OF THE GOLDEN WEST

AS A TRIBUTE TO THE ENGINEERING GENIUS
WHICH GAVE TO THE STATE OF CALIFORNIA
THE GOLDEN GATE BRIDGE
THE LONGEST BRIDGE SPAN IN THE WORLD
WE THE NATIVE SONS OF THE GOLDEN WEST
MAKE THIS DEDICATION
IN RECOGNITION OF
THE BEAUTY AND THE UTILITY
OF THIS GREAT STRUCTURE
AND THE SCIENTIFIC ACHIEVEMENT
FOR WHICH IT STANDS
MAY 27 1937

ONE HUNDRED AND FIFTEEN FEET SOUTHWARD FROM THIS PANEL ON THE CENTER
OF THE BRIDGE A STARRED DISK OF BRONZE MARKS THE CENTER OF THE OLD
CONTROL STATION OF BATTERY LANCASTER WHICH ONCE OCCUPIED THAT SITE
THAT POINT THE FIRST RECONNAISSANCE OF THE GOLDEN GATE BRIDGE WAS INITIA

TEOTIHUACAN

This ancient city belongs to the great classical period of the Indian civilization of Central America. The exceptional site on which it stands, 25 miles from Mexico City, was founded and inhabited by Totomac groups, originally from the Gulf, about whom little is known. These were followed by the Toltecs and then the Aztecs.

The Pyramid of the Sun, the Avenue of the Dead and lastly the Pyramid of the Moon are thought to have been built in the first century AD, or about the same time as the Antonine period in Rome. The urban complex of Teotihuacan, which is now being excavated, covers more than 58 square miles, of which no more than 1 1/2 square miles are taken up by the religious center. The proportions of the religious structures are, however, quite gigantic. The Avenue of the Dead, wrongly so named by the Aztecs, who thought that the mounds along either side must have been the tombs of ancient kings, gives some idea of those massive proportions: it was 2 1/2 miles long and 147 ft wide.

The Pyramid of the Sun is the most important structure at Teotihuacan. With sides of 1,140 ft, it is only sightly smaller than the Pyramid of Cheops in Egypt, from which it differs, however, in that it is flatter, rising to a height of only 245 ft. Its shape is more reminiscent of the *ziggurats* of Mesopotamia. It consumed more than a million cubic yards of stone, arranged around a central core of bricks, and must have been covered with a cladding of red mortar and flagstones.

The recent discovery, at its base, of a well and a tunnel 325 ft long leading to a cavity shaped like four petals under the center of the pyramid, poses a number of baffling questions about the cultural rites of the builders. Was this a royal hypogeum, an oracular grotto or a place where the skins of flayed human victims were stored?

Mexico. The ruins of Teotihuacan and the stairway of the Pyramid of the Sun.

Tula, the capital of the Toltecs, was founded in the 10th century, after the destruction of Teotihuacan by barbarous tribes from the north known as the Chichimecs.

The pyramid of Tlahuizcalpantecuhtli, situated in the middle of the ruins, is clearly unlike those of Teotihuacan. First of all, it is smaller: 130 ft square and only 33 ft high. Moreover, its base is surrounded by a forest of columns in the form of enormous porticoes, as later at Chichen-Itza. The structure of the temple which it supported was highly original: its pediment was borne by four sculpted pillars, the *atlantes,* crude images of the warriors who were the strength and the soul of the warrior state. With their grim features and feather head-dresses, their loincloths held up by a buckle symbolizing the setting sun, their sandals adorned with plumed serpents and their *atlatl,* or spear thrower, which together with a small sword formed their traditional arms, they symbolized the harsh, pitiless and fundamentally military civilization to which they belonged.

Thanks to an abundance of cotton and maize, the Toltecs during the reign of Tezcathipoca achieved unrivalled prosperity: their palaces were decorated with gold, jade, precious stones and sculpted friezes depicting jaguars, pumas and plumed serpents.

Human sacrifices were instituted as a means of thanking the gods for their generosity. This accounts for the ubiquitous *chac-mool,* curious statues of reclining human figures holding a tray on their bellies: it was here that the priests placed the heart of each sacrificial victim, the blood flowing away down small specially designed grooves.

Another innovation which occurs as a kind of *leitmotiv* at all Toltec sites, is the ritual ball court, in the shape of two opposing Ts—the setting for a strange game in which the prize was to see a member of the losing side beheaded with an obsidian knife.

Nowhere else was the gods' lust for blood as great as here; indeed a slightly sinister feeling pervades the ruins even today, as the visitors perceives, beyond the beauty of the monuments themselves, traces of the rituals of blood and death which lay hidden behind these plumed stones.

Mexico. The temple referred to as that of the Morning Star with, opposite, some of its giants.

Chichen-Itza ('the well of the Itza'), situated near the Yucatan coast on a cleared plain, was probably founded towards 435 AD. Such an arid and flat landscape would not seem at first sight to lend itself to a major settlement; in fact there was a drinking water supply, obtained from the *cenotes,* natural wells which collected rainwater. The city was quite large, covering more than 750 acres. Its history can be divided into two periods, and almost two cultures, which were quite different.

From 435 to 987 the population was purely Mayan in origin and culture, in the style of Palenque. After 987, the exiled king of Tula, Quetzalcoatl, took refuge there and gradually imposed a strict military Toltec culture. Entering a period of decline after 1190, the population built no more new monuments, and neglected those of the past, until the Spanish conquerors came and occupied the site.

The archeological area is so vast and the monuments are so scattered that one has to make a firm choice: the Pyramid of Kukulkan, the Temple of the Warriors, the Ball Court and the Sacred Well, all of which are grouped together south of the road. The remains on the other side are numerous, but not very spectacular, with the possible exception of the Caracol (Snail Shell) Tower, which is generally regarded as the finest Mayan observatory which has survived to modern times.

The pyramid-temple of Kukulkan, inaccurately known as El Castillo, has a base 180 ft square, and four steep flights of stairs leading to a sanctuary adorned with snake-like columns.

The Temple of the Warriors, which is preceded and surrounded by the forest of columns of its porticoes, is located on top of a second pyramid which is only 25 ft square.

The Ball-Court at Chichen-Itza is among the best-preserved samples of its kind in Mexico. The playing area is shaped like two opposing Ts, and the walls are clad with an abundance of sculpted ritual reliefs. It is the only such court which still has its stone ring intact. A highly realistic low relief gives us an idea of the rigor which attached to what is sometimes called a game, though it was really more of a religious ceremony. The object was to hit the ball, symbolizing the sun, through the stone ring, using only the joints (shoulders, elbows, knees and hips). The captain of the losing side was privileged to be publicly beheaded with a heavy obsidian cutlass.

Nearby is the Wall of the Skulls, on which only symbolic low reliefs are to be seen today, whereas it once served for the display of severed heads.

The small nearby site of Sayil has a highly unusual restored Mayan palace. This enormous structure, 275 ft long, consists of three recessed floors. The remarkable thing about it is the superb sculptures which adorn the façades of each floor, which can be reached by a monumental flight of stairs.

The Mayan temples of Sayil and Chichen-Itza.

SACSAHUAMAN

Clinging to a hilltop north of Cuzco, the amazing fortress of Sacsahuaman extends its powerful mass above the Inca capital which it was once required to defend. With its gigantic megalithic blocks, it is the most formidable citadel of the whole of pre-Columbian America.

It is still spectacular today, despite the fact that the Spaniards used many of its stones to build their colonial city; yet, curiously, little is known about this mysterious defensive structure. The date of its construction, in particular, is unknown. It was most probably built in several phases, perhaps at the beginning of the Inca period (14th century) in the case of the oldest northern and western sections, while it seems likely that the rest of the building dates from the period just before the arrival of the Spaniards, at the end of the Inca period.

In any case, this was an ambitious and challenging venture. According to some sources,

the Inca Tupac Ypangui, successor of the legendary Pachacutei, the founder of the Inca State as we know it, used more than 20,000 workers to transport and assemble the gigantic blocks of which the fortress is made. They probably used the same methods as those used by the Egyptians in building the pyramids—rollers, sleds, ramps of hard fill and sisal ropes, together with a massive workforce. The sheer scale of the fortress is staggering. In the legend, the first Inca, Manco Capac, was created on the shores of Lake Titicaca by Viracocha, his god, who promptly plunged him into the lake water and had him emerge near Cuzco, his future capital.

Why could not Viracocha have assembled these monstrously large stone blocks? The Spanish conquerors, who felt that only devils could have achieved such a super-human feat, must have been strongly tempted to believe that he did.

The ramparts consist of three enclosing walls of Cyclopean dimensions, carefully built in a zigzag pattern—much in the style of the great

French fortress-builder Vauban, centuries later. This layout forced any attacking force to expose its flank to the archers, slingers or spear-throwers defending the citadel. The enormous fortified outer wall enclosed several buildings and was reinforced by three massive round towers. One of them, richly adorned with precious stones and gold, must have been used as accomodation by an Inca when visiting the citadel. The other contained a water-tank kept constantly filled by water

Peru. The Incan fortress of Sacsahuaman seen from two different angles.

piped from an underground spring—a great boon during times of siege.

This overwhelming set of defensive structures, which is unique in the pre-Columbian civilizations, was accessible only by three narrow gates which could be sealed tight in case of danger by a heavy stone slab which fitted so perfectly into the wall that it became invisible and therefore secure against attack.

Sacsahuaman never fell to indigenous attackers; indeed the Spaniards had a hard time dislodging Manco Capac, in 1543, during a painful siege which took the life of Juan, the brother of Pizarro.

The enormous esplanade in front of the fortress was doubtless used for the ritual ceremonies of the cult of the sun, the *intirayim,* during the winter solstice. Nowadays these colorful festivities are performed once again, to the delight of the crowds of tourists, massed along the ramparts where the warriors of the Inca once stood guard.

BRASILIA

When elected president of Brazil in 1956, the first thing Rafael Kubitschek did was to plan the creation of a new capital city. The idea had been in the air since 1891, with the emphasis on the need for a capital closer to the center of the country, replacing Rio de Janeiro, which was felt to be too intimately associated with the coastal region. The projected transfer to the high plateaux of the hinterland had actually been adopted by a vote as early as 1895—only to be buried by oblivion and the passage of time.

In his decision on the matter, the new president even set a deadline—1960, the last year of his term of office. Twenty-six projects were produced in response to a competition; the winner was the Brazilian urban planner Lucio Costa. The architect Oscar Niemeyer was placed in charge of the construction of buildings, Le Corbusier was consulted, and work on the city began.

Between 1956 and 1960 the arid, windswept upland plateau, 3,600 feet above sea level, became a gigantic construction site. The land had to be surveyed, drains had to be dug and new roads had to be built, linking Brasilia to the main cities of Brazil and opening up vast expanses of territory to the outside world.

Over an area of more than 12,500 acres, 80,000 laborers worked round the clock, using 400,000 bags of cement per month and moving more than two million cubic feet of earth every day. In three years the principal features of the capital had been formed: on 21 April 1960, the National Day and anniversary of the discovery of Brazil by the Portuguese navigator Cabral, the President officially inaugurated the new capital, to which the principal government offices had already been transferred. His gamble had paid off.

Costa's brilliant design for the site blended perfectly into the landscape, which included a

crescent-shaped lake. Two immense avenues meet at right angles: the shorter of them (five miles long and 525 ft. wide) is set aside for official buildings. The longer one (8 miles long), the main thoroughfare of the residential areas, sweeps around in a curve following that of the lake. The point at which they meet is the hub of the entire city, with immense galleries housing restaurants, cinemas, playgrounds and playing fields, and a bus station with services to the whole of Brazil.

In this majestic and visionary setting, Oscar Niemeyer was given a free hand in the design of the public buildings. In this the followed his own genius and the sophisticated yet fervent lyricism inherent in his personality.

At the edger of the lake, the Alvorada Palace (Palace of the Dawn), symbolizing the brillant future of Brazil, is the private residence of the president of the Republic. The astonishing lightness and refinement of this glass building, which is reflected in the waters of the pool, graced by Ceschiatti's water-nymphs, are due to the use of elegant lozenge-shaped pillars.

The Plaza of the Three Powers is the most famous part of the civic center of Brasilia. It consists of an immense triangular platform, where official parades take place, and at the corners of which stand the buildings of the highest organs of the State. At the top of the triangle, towards the lake, the Palace of the Congress represents the legislature. It is a gallery 655 ft. long and 260 wide, built in the form of an infrastructure and housing all the services of the respective chambers.

The Chamber of Deputies is crowned by the upper half of a concrete sphere 260 ft. in diameter, while the structure which stands over the Chamber of the Senate is the lower half of a similar sphere. Twin towers containing administrative offices stand in the midst of this remarkable arrangement of shapes.

At the base of the triangle the other

branches of power stand face to face. The Executive takes the form of a very stark government palace, with a strictly horizontal roof and eighteen graceful concrete pillars.

Apart from these official buildings there are only two other structures along the 'Monumental Axis': the theater, a simple truncated pyramid, and the cathedral, which is without a doubt the most extraordinary building in the whole of Brasilia. It consists of an astonishing sheaf of stylized concrete elements, sharply curved towards the middle, rather like a cluster of huge boomerangs. Linked by panels of rafractory glass, they give the sanctuary the silhouette of a huge transparent crown, its points soaring skywards, more than 130 feet above the ground.

The sacristy and baptistry are both under ground, as is the entrance—strange catacombs leading to the luminous interior of this mystical shape, which can accomodate a congregation of four thousand. The floor level is a circle 230 feet in diameter. The side chapels are arranged against the walls, with no partitions whatsoever, in a deliberate attempt to break with the traditional divisions of religious space. In the same spirit, aluminium angels, suspended from the ceiling, constitute a new approach to sacred sculpture. The magnificence, purity and spiritual exaltation which radiate from this remarkable building could only be those of a house of God.

Such is Brasilia, the product of political will and architectural genius combined. In this city, which has been planned to the nth degree, everything has been studied, programmed and provided for. Is it merely a symbol and a admirable work of art? Or will it also be, in the words of the man who made it, a city "for free men, who feel life in its greatness and its fragility, and who value simple and pure things"?

Brasilia. Monumental Avenue, the "Pioneers" Statue, and Parliament.

EASTER ISLAND

The giant stone statues of Easter Island would be impressive and awesome even if they were surrounded by the palaces and temples of the ancient capital of some rich and powerful civilization. But they seem nothing short of miraculous in the desolate surroundings in which they occur. Easter Island is the loneliest place on earth: a barren vocanic island, barely twice the size of Manhattan, thousands of miles out into the Pacific.

The famous statues—the *Moai*—are actually elongated, long-eared busts, all made in virtually the same style. When the Easter Island civilization was at its height, probably between the 12th and late 17th centuries, they were erected in rows usually facing inland, on large numbers of stone-platform mausoleums *(ahu)* dotted around the coast. From the logbook of Admiral Roggeveen, the Dutchman who first discovered the island, we know that they were still standing and being venerated in 1722; but by the time Captain Cook arrived in 1774 most of them had been overthrown in a civil war which had decimated the population.

All of the statues were carved from the soft yellow-grey tuff in the crater walls of the Rano-Raraku volcano, in the eastern corner of the island. About half of them, in varying stages of completion, are still standing either inside the quarries or just outside the rim of the crater. Besides those which formerly towered above the coastal mausoleums, a small number of isolated statues were embedded directly in the ground in various parts of the island.

Using primitive stone picks, the sculptors cut out and polished the front and sides, detaching the back from the bedrock last of all; the statue was then moved away to an area downhill from the crater, where the back was finished. Only after it had been erected on the *ahu* was it given its final awesome appearance: deep oval eye sockets were added and a massive cylinder of red vocanic rock, the *pukao*, or topknot, was placed on its head. At least some of the statues were originally painted white and red.

The size of the *Moai* is astounding: the largest of those formerly erected on an *ahu* was 32 feet tall and weighed 80 tons, with a *pukao* of some 11 tons perched on its head. The largest of those standing guard outside the crater rim is some 37 feet tall, and the biggest incomplete *Moai* still in the quarry stands the height of a seven—storey house—68 feet!

Nowadays it is only possible to visualize the majestic rows of these huge monoliths each capped by a *pukao*, towering over the enormous stone platforms of the mausoleums, their backs turned to the ocean. Civil war has ruined most of these statues; some others have fallen into the sea as a result of erosion. The great Tonga-Riki *ahu*, not far from the quarries, was virtually swept away by the tidal wave which struck Easter Island after the Chilean earthquake of 1960. All of the *ahu* statues have been exposed for centuries to the fierce winds and driving rains which lash the island for months at a time.

Assorted views ofthe intriguing mammoth statues on Easter Island.

TAJ MAHAL

On the bank of the Yamana, a tributary of the Ganges which once fed the irrigation canals of the rich Agra plain, stands the Taj Mahal, perhaps the most enchanting and perfect building of 17th-century Moghul India.

It is an expression, in white marble, of the overwhelming grief of the Moghul Emperor Shah-Jahan over the death of his wife Muntaz Mahal ("the chosen one of the harem") giving birth to her ninth child. The sovereign, who was aged 39 at the time, decided to build in her honor this prodigious funerary mosque in order to immortalize her memory and their love.

For 16 years, from 1632 to 1648, 20,000 masons, marble sculptors and artists toiled relentlessly to produce this gem, under the guidance of several architects, including a Venetian, a Turk (a pupil of the great Simal) and a Frenchman, Augustin de Bordeaux. Their collaboration led to the creation of an exceptional monument, a veritable symphony of diaphanous milky-white marble, of unreal purity and grandiose and harmonious proportions. It is a heart-rending

outburst of faith, a cry to heaven.

Surrounded by the immense gardens (43 acres) of Shah-Jahan across which runs a "sacred avenue" paved with red sandstone, and reflected in a long turquoise pool directly in front of it, the Taj Mahal eclipses everything. It has an enchanting, fascinating presence which obsesses one to the exclusion of all else.

The mausoleum, which is built on a marble terrace 305 feet square, is in the classical Iranian style, since the empress belonged to the small Persian colony which was a part of the aristocratic elite of imperial India. The layout is based on a square with sides of 185 feet and flattened corners; an extraordinary bulbous dome 58 feet in diameter and 192 high crowns the entire structure like a brilliant, translucid halo.

Each of the four main faces has an enormous *iwan*—a tall, wide porch above which there is a semi-cupola with bee-hive pendants typical of the Islamic architecture of Persia. The central cupola is framed by four delicate minarets, which reach up to heaven like a prayer.

The decoration of the tomb is particularly sumptuous and original. It consists largely of

finely sculpted marble sometimes enhanced by semi-precious stones in the form of geometric arabesques, floral garlands and Kufic calligraphy reproducing verses from the Koran.

Sober, delicate and refined, yet at the same time exuberant, this ornamentation runs along porches, entwines itself around columns and girdles tympani in anincredible and lavish outpouring of luminous love and hope.

This building embodies not only the elegant perfection of the great classical architecture and the marvelous ornamental profusion of the Persian sanctuaries, but also the quivering emotion of the greatest works of Romanticism. In it the plain human love of a man has culminated in an artistic masterpiece and an overwhelming mystical utterance. In it, passion proves to be a wonderful vehicle for both beauty and faith.

India. The Taj Mahal in Agra. Left: close-up of a corner of the shrine. Opposite: the fountains.

It was originally intended that the emperor would be buried in a black Taj Mahal across the river, facing the tomb of his loved one. The state of the kingdom's finances, however, made this impossible, so he joined her in the funerary chamber of the mausoleum.

At one time a golden grill highlighted with sapphires and diamonds used to seal the entrance to the sarcophagi. Financial trouble, however, obliged the son and successor of Shah Jahan to sell this treasure so as to raise funds with which to quell a provincial rebellion. In exchange he commissioned a white marble balustrade, carved in a delicate lattice-work pattern, which can still be seen.

But it is in the serene and secret half-light of the crypt that the true tombs are venerated, in the form of a few bones placed in two far less spectacular and intimate caskets.

In the setting sun, at dawn or by moonlight, the Taj Mahal seems to assume the transparence of a dream, and its marble, which one normally thinks of as cold, takes on different hues: livid, pink, bluish or fair, it seems to tremble in celestial light and come to life.

KONARAK

This amazing and wholly extraordinary monument still commands admiration and inspires awe. The gigantic ruins of an ornate and immense chariot lie half-buried in sand, at an isolated spot on a beach in the Gulf of Bengal. This is one of the most famous Brahman temples in India, dedicated to Surya, the god of the sun, by King Marasimba I (1238-1264), who wanted this monumental work to be as unusual as it was sumptuous.

Unusual it certainly is, being a temple conceived as a solar chariot drawn by 7 horses. And sumptuous, too, by virtue of the exceptional quality of the remarkable sculpted ornaments which decorate it. Its royal builder took the further bold step of choosing as a site a sandy spot 2 miles from the sea.

This ambitious gamble did not entirely pay off because, although the building is certainly considered as a gem of Indian decorative architecture, it has taken a severe beating, over the centuries, from the ever-present sea air and is now in a distinctly ruined state. Moreover, crushed under the weight of its mass of ochre stone, it is gradually sinking into the sand.

Nonetheless it is still a disconcerting manifestation of human faith, and obviously owes its existence to men of superlative spirit, imagination and originality. This silhouette, massive and at the same time fragile, touching yet undoubtedly the work of a megalomaniac, makes an unforgettable and deeply impressive sight, anchored in the sand so close to the ocean.

This colossal structure excites enthusiasm as well as admiration. On each of its faces there are 12 immense wheels, 10 ft in diameter, which form the chariot of the sun, symbolically drawn by 6 gigantic animals over 6 ft tall: two lions

attacking elephants, 2 elephants, and 2 horses subduing fantastic animals. Even more astounding are the series of low reliefs, finely carved and wrought like items of rare jewelry, which run all along the walls and between the wheels, weaving an incredible tapestry of stone in which the whole of the Hindu bestiary is summarized.

In the company of dancers, musicians and sacred courtesans, the fantastic lions and serpents dance their way through a hallucinating marble sabbat, while Surya, the resplendent sun, presides over this outpouring of his own mythology.

Three flights of stairs, each framed by a pair of colossal animals, lead to the upper floor.

Konarak is one of the most formidable examples of that "sculpted architecture" in which decoration determines form. Laden, and even overladen with decorative work, with a naive symbolic allegory which could easily have been in poor taste, this ruined edifice is quite simply grandiose, admirable, and moreover unique.

India. Two perspectives on the Temple of the Sun in Konarak. Right: the crowning portion of the Kapaliswa Temple in Madras.

AJANTA

These sculpted grottoes take us into the unreal and legendary world of Buddhism: the mural frescoes, the low-reliefs and even the breath-taking architecture which has been literally carved like a negative into the rock face, are a hymn in stone in honor of the Buddha.

There are two distinct types of building carved in the rock: the monasteries *(vihars)* which house a small monastic community, and the temples *(shaitya)*, in which the godhead was venerated and exalted. They were made during two periods: the oldest in the second and first centuries BC, and the most recent between the third and the sixth centuries AD. All of them remained occupied until the eighth century.

The Ajanta grottoes are situated in the ravine of the Vaghora River, deep in the Indhyadri Mountains, 300 miles from Bombay. There are 30 of them all told, carved out of a volcanic rock not unlike basalt and opening on the rock face of the gorge itself. There are only five temples, whereas the monasteries in which the Buddhist monks used to live total 25. The layout of traditional buildings built on flat ground in the normal manner is faithfully reproduced here: a vestibule, a hall for prayer and an apse containing a stupa carved in the rock.

Excavation was carried out from an axial gallery, carved out with pickaxes and bars, which could then be enlarged and given the desired shape. The façade was sculpted after the rock face had been smoothed out, whereas the ceilings were all excavated in the form of vaults.

Rather than the nature of the site and the meaning of the grottoes, it is its ornamentation which makes Ajanta one of the finest pieces of religious art in the world. As the centuries passed, the sculptures, all of which are noble and refined, and the paintings—frescoes would be a better term —became more and more sumptuous and brilliant.

The ones in the oldest grottoes are plain, stark and sometimes crude—an austere and simple expression of homage, full of solid and touching faith.

The artwork in the later sanctuaries is an outpouring of mystical exuberance, an ornamental explosion full of vitality and joy. Faith has here become happy and enthusiastic—the standard of Buddhism being proudly brandished by

the artist for his God to see.

Such an abundance of superb low-reliefs and paintings must have cost a lot of money. They were, in fact, financed by large gifts made to the monastic communities which, being required by their vows to live very frugally, used these resources in order to make their sanctuaries as sumptuously ornate as possible.

These splendid reliefs, as well as the frescoes, which are among the most beautiful of the Buddhist world, are largely devoted to the life of the Buddha. The walls are covered with scenes which emphasize the kindness, serenity and moral beauty of the *bodhisattvas,* (literally, "those who possess quality"). This name was given to the various incarnations of the Buddha in his previous lives, and also to "wise men" who worked for the good of mankind and whose lives were an example for others. The most famous of these is *Blue Lotus Bodhisattva* adorning the end wall of grotto No. 1, which is one of the finest.

Yet the artists of the later sanctuaries, which were painted at the height of the Gupta civilization, sometimes included exquisite figures or the faces of ordinary mortals alongside their religious themes. The *Princess at her Toilet,* an evanescent and highly modest ancestor of Velasquez's *Venus with a Mirror,* is a good example of this kind of secular figure, all of which were depicted with features ennobled by grace, purity and innocence.

Although these works constitute a kind of Buddhist cathechism, with a strong dogmatic content, the quality of the artistry, the magic of the colors and the delicate poetry of the paintings are such that, Buddhist or not, the visitor tends to be spellbound by this fantastic testimony of a radiant Hindu Buddhism.

In the hollows of these grottoes which were hewn out of the rock by living faith, on these walls which were so laboriously flattened and covered with a pathetic coating of chopped straw, manure and molasses, one can see one of the most exceptional accomplishments of pictorial art.

India. The sculpted Buddhist grottos of Ajanta. Opposite: the peristyle greeting the visitor to Grotto No. 1.

ANGKOR

The famous ruins lie deep in the forest, on the territory of ancient Cambodia, of which they are the most important archeological site. They were widely publicized by the colonial exposition of 1931 and celebrated by French novelist Pierre Loti; in fact the artistry of the ancient Khmer sculptors had so identified the image of the temple with that of the country that they even appeared on the old Cambodian flag.

However, there are thousands of monuments in the Cambodian forests and the term *angkor* applies to many structures of different periods, styles and qualities.

About the year 790 a Javanese prince settled in the region, achieving the political unity of the Khmer people. Angkor was founded as a capital by Yasovarman I (889-900) on the site of an earlier city. For more than 5 centuries, the Khmer kings, who were great builders, erected a

succession of palaces and temples which gradually came to form an original style of architecture and decorative sculpture.

Despite its size and complexity, the site of Angkor is in itself a summary of Khmer art, of which it is the finest synthesis and the most grandiose illustration. Among the countless structures, in a more or less ruined condition, which lie strewn about the forest, there are two large groups which are still highly spectacular and representative.

Angkor Vat was a religious city, a kind of monastic temple, whose perfect balance and harmonious proportions make it unquestionably a masterpiece. Built in 1122 by Suryavarman II, and surrounded by a broad ditch as well as a surrounding wall three miles long, it can be reached by a paved roadway 715 ft. long, bordered by statues, which crosses the moats.

The temple, which is a model of orderly layout and symmetry, rests on a base 780 feet square, consisting of a high open gallery, the wall of which is sculpted throughout its entire length and forms a marvelous stone fresco running right

around the building. The life of the king, the legend of Rama, the story of Khrisma and scenes from war and courtly life are depicted on it in very flat low-reliefs, covering more than half an acre, which were originally painted bright colors.

Though brilliantly designed, the architecture is somewhat disappointingly executed at times. The use of blocks of sandstone weighing as much as several tons is certainly a remarkable feat; but they were merely squared off and assembled without cement, so that they were kept in place only by gravity. Hasty work done particularly during the 12th and 13th centuries made them vulnerable to the climate, to roots,

Cambodia. A broad view of the Temple of Angkor Vat. Opposite: the main courtyard. Left: the sculpted suggestion of the four faces of a Bodisattva king.

water seepage and the action of seeds germinating in the cracks.

Khmer art, which was at first influenced by India and Java, quickly found its own characteristic personal style. The themes of the sandstone carvings are the same everywhere: mythology and legendary stories, depicting, *inter alia,* the *Asparas,* the sacred dancing girls and courtesans, and the *Devatas,* their daughters. Ornamentation is essentially repetitive. Though graceful and lively at first, the figures became monotonous and stiff after the 12th century. The later temples contain too many impersonal friezes, sometimes poorly reproduced in mediocre stereotyped series.

Even so, there was still vigor, grace and captivating sensitivity in the long strips of sculpted scenes at Angkor-Vat. The dancing girls seemed to come to life and quiver when the Cambodian village girls went to caress their already glossy stone breasts in the hope of achieving high fertility. And in the evenings, catching the short-lived golden glow of the setting sun, the celestial *Asparas* seemed once again to enliven the long garlands of rust-colored stone.

THE FORBIDDEN CITY

Until the 1912 revolution this symbolic title was applied to the old imperial city and its palace. Among the ordinary people it was known as the Purple City, purple being the color of the polar star; accordingly it meant that the emperor's residence was the cosmic center of ancient China and of the famous Middle Kingdom.

In the heart of the ancient Ming capital it was the holy of holies of the all-powerful State, and as such was obviously out of bounds, on pain of death, to anyone not authorized to work in the service of the palace. In the eyes of the rest of the world, it was moreover for many centuries the quintessence of traditional China: a triumph of 15th-century Chinese architecture and a fascinating image of the splendor and fairy-tale wonders of a legendary Orient, both rich and plain, opulent and serene, cruel and refined.

The enclosure of the imperial palace—a veritable administrative city—occupied an area of 180 acres, surrounded by a 33 ft wall with bastions at its four corners and an outer moat, 160 ft wide, which further enhanced its sacred and invulnerable appearance.

The Forbidden City is highly complex, as it contains more than 9,000 rooms distributed

Peking. The Temple of the Heavens and two of the buildings contained within the Forbidden City.

among 25 palaces or pavilions reached by 10 monumental doors and a half-dozen large court-yards. But it is also very simple in the sense that it can be broken up into a major axis of structures arranged in rows, and two wings which contain the administrative buildings of the State. The six major palaces are themselves divided into 3 formal buildings intended for political and public relations and 3 more discreet buildings which housed the private residence of the emperor and his spouse.

Wherever one looks there are marvelous gardens (only 20% of the total area is built on), the purple of walls, the undulating roofs of the pagodas with their glazed hues, a profusion of sculpted marble, the delight of splashing water and an accumulation of vast wealth: thrones, perfume-burners consuming sandalwood and pine, gilded decorative work, mosaics, low reliefs, etc.

The sublime serenity and refinement of this privileged sanctuary, with its exquisite scents and splashing fountains contrasted violently with

the harsh treatment which the imperial regime meted out to its own citizens and the grim struggle for survival which was the lot of the common people. The gently poetic and idyllic names given to each of the palaces were whole worlds apart from the terrible living conditions of medieval China. This gilded corner of Paradise was truly separate from the passage of time, and was totally and deliberately excluded from the miseries and afflictions of ordinary men.

All the structures within the Forbidden City were built between 1407 and 1420 by the Ming rulers; they were much restored in later centuries, as a result of numerous disastrous fires, so that the present state of the palaces is more or less as it was in the 18th century.

The political part of the palace comprises 3 pavilions separated by 2 courtyards to which access is provided by monumental gates. The first courtyard contains a meandering stream which follows a carefully laid out course in the shape of a bow, with 5 marble bridges symbolizing the 5 virtues.

The largest hall, known as Supreme Har-mony (162 ft by 100) was the throne room, for use during receptions. A splendid gilded ceiling still stands, 90 ft above the ground, on 24 gilded columns adorned with dragons.

The private part of the palace was on a more modest, homely scale: the Ming emperors used to sleep in the Room of Celestial Purity. The empress, however, had her throne in the *kiaotai* room, while the Pavilion of Earthly Tranquility served as her personal quarters.

During the Ming period, 9,000 women (including 3 wives, 6 favorites and as many as 2,000 concubines) and 70,000 eunuchs lived in the other parts of the City, in the pavilions and rooms of the lateral parts.

These figures and the fabulous treasures (gems, precious stones, objects of jade, amber, gold or ivory) accumulated by the thousand in rooms which have now become museums are a distant reflection of the unreal and inhuman splendor which has held the world spellbound for centuries.

THE GREAT WALL OF CHINA

This phenomenal serpent of earth, erected in the mountains, is the only human structure which can be seen from the moon.

At a time when the 'warring kingdoms' kept China in a fragmented state (5th century BC), each small state protected itself against its neighbors by means of long defensive walls. This was particularly true of their northern frontiers, where they were anxious to deter the hordes which regularly swept out of Mongolia.

When the Huang dynasty reunified this host of scattered provinces into an empire, a common defensive line had to be built. The Huang emperor then decided to join up these segments of loosely arranged wall to form a system of continuous fortifications. For 10 years, under the Huang, 300,000 men labored to complete the common wall. Under the Han this continuous wall was developed and extended until it was a veritable stone rampart, comparable to the *lines* of the Romans, along the northern frontiers.

As a result of political and military shifts of fortune late in the 16th century—the frontiers having first slipped south and later moved north—the wall found itself within the territory of a single state, thus losing any strategic importance it

might have had. It was therefore almost completely abandoned. But when the Ming, in the 14th century, drove back the Mongols, they had to restore the northern frontiers by consolidating it.

Between 1368 and 1500 it gradually assumed its present shape. For nearly 7 1/2 thousand miles, divided into 9 military and administrative commands, it protected the northern and western frontiers, at the edge of Mongolia and the Gobi Desert. From the time of the Ts'ing onwards it gradually fell into ruin, only a few segments—those which can be visited today—remaining intact.

The height of the wall vall varies from 23 to 26 ft; it is about 20 ft thick at the base and a little less at the top. It consists of 2 thick outer stone walls around a core of earth and rocks. The rampart walk, which is interrupted by crude flights of stairs to compensate for changes in the terrain, was strengthened by 2,500 stone towers, each of which had 2 floors: the first floor was used as a guard room, while the terrace on the second was reserved for the lookout. Battlements were on one side only, the one from which it was assumed that the enemy would come. In many delicate strategic centers, however, the wall was doubled, and certain exposed stretches had as many as ten parallel ramparts.

Following only the ridges and peaks of the particularly mountainous provinces which it was required to defend, the wall twisted and turned in its spectacular course from peak to peak. Although it was intended mainly as a military and defensive structure, it also provided a rapid means of communication: its rampart walk, which could let 5 horsemen ride abreast, was used by imperial messengers and the caravans which, in hostile areas, found that it afforded them safety and ease of movement.

Today the part of the wall which is most easily accessible and best restored is about 25 miles west of Peking. It is about 1.400 years old, having been built in the 6th century AD and altered during the Ming period. Visitors can see a tower, two concentric ramparts and a fine gate adorned with sculpted Buddhas, dating from 1439.

With a little imagination it is still possible to visualize the Ming soldiers, scanning the steppe towards the northwest, fervently hoping that they were not about to see an immense cloud of dust stirred up in the distance by aggressive hordes of Mongol horsemen.

China. Two views of the Great Wall, near Peking.

JAPANESE SANCTUARIES

Japan—the land of concrete, the economic miracle, violent protest and slot machines—is actually one of those countries where mysticism and religion are most deeply rooted in daily life. Whether it be the art of flower arrangement, the tea ceremony, the cult of the garden or even the ritual of spectacular suicides, everything speaks of the fundamental importance of metaphysical concerns. In the midst of the frenzied din of an outpouring of industrial exuberance, the Japanese still know how to seek out a quiet corner for peace and meditation.

The oldest religion of Japan is Shinto, a pantheistic animism in which the forces of nature —water, springs, rocks, trees—are venerated. In a sense, therefore, the whole of nature itself is the biggest Shinto temple. Among the more typical examples of Shinto religious architecture, the sanctuaries of Izuno, Ise and Itsukushima are the most venerable and the most spectacular.

Ise and Izuno are the oldest. The temples are built on a thick wooden platform supported by a stout central pillar, symbolizing the axis of the universe, which is also found on primitive huts.

The sanctuary of Itsukushima, 12 ½ miles from Hiroshima, conforms to the traditional principles of Shinto architecture and is one of the most remarkable examples of the perfect blend between temple and nature. Built entirely on piles, not far off shore in a small bay, it is transformed by each high tide into an unreal and quite extraordinary mirage which seems to be floating on the waves.

Buddhist temples flourished everywhere. They are the transposition of the Chinese monasteries: a vast rectangular cloister surrounding an empty area in which the *kondo* (golden pavilion) containing the Buddha, used to stand. This is a graceful pagoda with several floors, resting on a platform paved with stone slabs. Finely curved columns with no capitals support the rest of the building; the roofs have the characteristic delicate curves. Built in honor of the Buddha, the *kondos* are always exceptionally well decorated.

At Nikko, on the island of Honshu, there is a group of Buddhist sanctuaries which offer a wholly different type of architecture and ornamentation. The most famous of these is the sanctuary-mausoleum of Tosho-gu.

SYDNEY OPERA HOUSE

"They drawings submitted are simple to the point of being diagrammatic. Nevertheless, we are convinced that they present a concept of an opera house which is capable of being one of the great buildings of the world." With these prophetic words, the judges pronounced 38-year-old Joern Utzon of Denmark the winner of the 1957 international competition for the design of the Sydney Opera House, from a field of 233 architects.

Despite the controversy which has surrounded the project, the glittering clusters of vaulted roofs which stand on their monumental podium at the entrance to Sydney Harbor now provide almost exactly what Premier Cahill had in mind when the project was first proposed in 1954:

Japan. Above: the temples of Itsukushima, on the island of Miyajima, and Kyoto. Below: the Kasuga and Nikko temples.
Last page: twin glimpses of the Sydney Opera House.

a worthy home for the performing arts in Australia, in a world-famous architectural setting.

Its name, however, is misleading, as opera is only one of its functions, and not the principal one. It is really a complex for the performing arts, ith many related facilities, yet the name Opera House, which had originally been used no doubt for convenience was later kept, partly for political reasons, after the nature of the project had been changed.

The three shell clusters of the Sydney Opera House—Concert Hall, Opera Theatre and Restaurant—rest on a huge granite-clad platform, known as the podium, which was inspired by the pre-Columbian temple platforms which Utzon had so greatly admired in Mexico.

The sensation of ascending into a special, exalted world is enhanced by the massive staircase —also borrowed from Mayan temple architecture —which extends the full width of the podium at the southern end. Once one is on the podium, with its intriguing interplay of space patterns, the skyward thrust of the roof vaults with their vertical ribbed patterns of ceramic tiles combines with the sight of sea, ships and sky to give one a curiously transcendental feeling of excitement.